CASTLE WETTERSTEIN

CASTLE WETTERSTEIN

Frank Wedekind

edited and translated by Ian Johnston

contextual materials edited and translated by Nisha Kommattam

broadview press

Broadview Press – www.broadviewpress.com
Peterborough, Ontario, Canada

Founded in 1985, Broadview Press remains a wholly independent publishing house. Broadview's focus is on academic publishing: our titles are accessible to university and college students as well as scholars and general readers. With over 600 titles in print, Broadview has become a leading international publisher in the humanities, with world-wide distribution. Broadview is committed to environmentally responsible publishing and fair business practices.

Library and Archives Canada Cataloguing in Publication

Title: Castle Wetterstein / Frank Wedekind ; edited and translated by Ian Johnston ; contextual materials compiled and translated by Nisha Kommattam.
Other titles: Schloss Wetterstein. English
Names: Wedekind, Frank, 1864-1918, author. | Johnston, Ian (Ian Courtenay), 1938- editor, translator.
Description: Translated from the German. | Translation of: Schloss Wetterstein.
Identifiers: Canadiana 20190094427 | ISBN 9781554814251 (softcover)
Classification: LCC PT2647.E26 S313 2019 | DDC 832/.8—dc23

Broadview Press handles its own distribution in North America:
PO Box 1243, Peterborough, Ontario, K9J 7H5, Canada
555 Riverwalk Parkway, Tonawanda, NY 14150, USA
Tel: (705) 743-8990; Fax: (705) 743-8353
email: customerservice@broadviewpress.com

Distribution is handled by Eurospan Group in the UK, Europe, Central Asia, Middle East, Africa, India, Southeast Asia, Central America, and the Caribbean. Distribution is handled by Footprint Books in Australia and New Zealand.

Broadview Press acknowledges the financial support of the Government of Canada for our publishing activities.

Canada

Staff Writer and Developmental Editor: Helena Snopek
Cover Designer: Lisa Brawn
Typesetter: Alexandria Stuart

PRINTED IN CANADA

Contents

Introduction

Frank (Benjamin Franklin) Wedekind 1864–1918

"At the beginning stands Wedekind." So wrote German literary critic Rudolf Kayser in 1917, writing of the new form of theatre flourishing in Germany as Expressionism was coming to dominate the arts. Though his name is little recognized today, in the first decades of the twentieth century Frank Wedekind was acknowledged by many artists and critics as being among the most important figures in the German avant-garde. The controversial subject matter of his plays brazenly challenged the social mores of Wilhelmine[1] Germany, expressing disdain for the repressive and commercial culture that had come to dominate the country in the wake of the rapid industrialization of the late nineteenth century. Although he faced frequent challenges and his work was often censored (especially at the beginning of his career), Wedekind nevertheless managed to build an enthusiastic audience and win profound respect for his writings, earning admiration from the likes of Bertolt Brecht. Since his death in 1918, his writings have provided inspiration for numerous films, operas, and even a Broadway rock musical.

Wedekind was born in Hanover in 1864 to a Swiss mother and German father. The family was quite well off; his father, Friedrich, was a doctor by profession, though he also worked extensively as a journalist and activist in support of liberal causes. Disappointed by the reactionary climate of 1850s Germany, he had emigrated to America, where he had worked as a physician both in Oakland and in San Francisco. Wedekind was born while the family was visiting Germany, and apparently received his unusual given names as a nod to his American ties as well as to Friedrich's democratic social

1 *Wilhelmine* The term is used to describe the period between 1890–1918, during which Germany was ruled by Emperor Wilhelm II.

views. (Wedekind carried American citizenship papers for most of his life; only with the onset of the First World War was he compelled to obtain a German passport.) The family never returned to America after Frank's birth, however, moving instead to Aarau in northern Switzerland, where the political climate was more congenial.

Friedrich encouraged his son to pursue a legal career, but Wedekind soon became dissatisfied with this path, and showed signs of wanting to write for a living. He moved to Zurich in 1886, finding employment at an advertising firm at which he composed advertisements for the soup brand Maggi and worked as a circus publicist. Wedekind continued at this position for about seven months before deciding to commit himself to freelance writing; but failing in this and finding himself in desperate financial straits, he returned to the law in 1887. Wedekind's father died within the subsequent year, and Wedekind was left with an inheritance that freed him up to pursue his writing once more.

It was about three years before Wedekind began writing his first play. Written in 1890–91, *Frühlings Erwachen*, or *Spring Awakening*, remains Wedekind's best known work, and is widely considered a seminal work in Expressionist theater and modern theater as a whole. In it Wedekind first expressed many of the themes that would come to define much of his career and, indeed, much of the work of the Expressionist playwrights overall. The play powerfully criticized much of what was central to late nineteenth-century German society—social conservatism, an educational system over-encumbered by tradition, and—most significantly for Wedekind—moral prudery and sexual repression. Subtitled *A Children's Tragedy*, the play centers on a group of teenagers struggling to come to terms with and confront the sexually repressive culture dominated by the adults in their lives. The script touches on topics such as masturbation, homosexuality, child abuse, rape, abortion, suicide, and atheism; parents and teachers are portrayed as grossly inept, oppressive, and at times downright cruel; the teenagers are their tragic victims. The play was remarkable for focusing on the liminal stage between childhood and adulthood—a stage whose existence had at this point been barely acknowledged in Western culture—and for treating the emotional lives of teenagers with seriousness. To some audiences at the time, the play's subtitle may have seemed almost an oxymoron.

Not surprisingly, *Spring Awakening* was met with accusations of obscenity; performances were banned for over a decade. After the ban was lifted in 1906, however, *Spring Awakening* became a standard in the rotation of many German theaters. Some critics have since come to see the play as a harbinger of the youth culture that exploded much later in the twentieth century. Despite the currents of controversy that have continued to swirl around the play, it was adapted as a film in 1929, and as a successful Broadway musical in 2006.

With *Spring Awakening* having earned him notoriety rather than immediate success, Wedekind's career continued to be unstable. He moved to Paris in 1891, where he lived the life of the bohemian avant-garde, visiting Parisian cabarets and music halls by day and frequenting brothels by night. His many sexual exploits were recorded in a detailed diary, released in English translation as *Diary of an Erotic Life* in 1990. Paris functioned as a kind of epicenter of many modern cultural trends that fascinated and frustrated Wedekind—among them the increasingly widespread commercialization of sex and the arts. These themes came to the forefront of Wedekind's next play, *Erdgeist* (1895). *Earth Spirit*, as it is usually translated, was the first of two plays centered on the character of Lulu, an orphaned young woman who is rescued from the streets by a wealthy newspaper entrepreneur (a character who Wedekind sometimes played himself) and who then becomes his mistress, after which she is traded to another man, and has affairs with numerous others. She is eventually killed by Jack the Ripper in the final scene of the sequel play. Like Wedekind's first play, both *Earth Spirit* and its sequel *Die Büchse der Pandora* (*Pandora's Box*, 1904) were considered by many to be obscene. The character of Lulu, whose inner nature is constantly misapprehended by the various men she encounters, is written to represent primal, erotic feminine energy. Some critics have seen the play as essentially misogynistic in its portrayal of female sexuality, while others have seen it as depicting a character struggling against a domineering society for her own sexual empowerment. Like *Spring Awakening*, the Lulu plays were brought to the screen in 1929; the film *Pandora's Box* starred the iconic silent film actress Louise Brooks.

By 1893 Wedekind's inheritance had run out. In dire straits financially, he became employed as secretary to an art dealer and forger named Willy Grétor; financial struggles would continue to be a recurring factor in Wedekind's life.

Returning to Germany in 1895, he attempted to find theaters willing to produce his plays. *Earth Spirit* premiered in Leipzig in 1898 (before a working-class audience who interpreted it largely as socialist propaganda). But Wedekind's plays would never provide him with a steady income; he found work writing content for *Simplicissimus*, a satirical journal founded by Albert Langen in 1896. Though Wedekind had little interest in politics of the sort emphasised in the journal, he contributed several politically oriented poems for the sake of financial gain, acting under the erroneous impression that his poems would be published only upon review by a lawyer. One of the poems—a satirical attack on the Emperor—attracted the notice of government authorities, and in 1898, shortly after the Munich premier of *Earth Spirit*, Wedekind received notice of his impending arrest. He fled briefly to Switzerland, where he began composing *Der Marquis von Keith* (which he later described as his best work). Wedekind returned to Germany after the new play's completion, where he was convicted of treason and imprisoned for a period of seven months beginning in 1899. Wedekind was blunt in speaking of his *Simplicissimus* work later in life:"with the hunger-lash," he said, "you can train your poets to adopt any viewpoint."

Wedekind's career took another turn following his release from prison in 1900: he was hired to work as a singer and guitarist in a Munich cabaret, *Die elf Scharfrichter*. Generally speaking, he did not enjoy the work. Believing that good art needed to be morally and intellectually stimulating as well as amusing, Wedekind felt the light entertainment of the cabaret to be beneath him. Nevertheless, his cabaret career was a success. He made more money from his performances here than he ever had yet from his writing, and, shrewdly, he used this success to push companies to produce his plays. Wedekind was noted for his bizarre performance style, which some described as simultaneously amateurish and charismatic, and he carried his cabaret experience over into his literary career, performing public readings of his works and frequently acting in productions of his own plays. In 1905 Wedekind starred as Jack the Ripper in a production of *Pandora's Box*, opposite a popular Austrian actress named Tilly Newes. Wedekind married Tilly—who was twenty-two years younger than him—the following year, becoming strictly monogamous as well as abusively jealous. The couple had two children but the relationship was highly tumultuous, leading Tilly to attempt suicide, and to try—unsuccessfully—to obtain a divorce.

Many of Wedekind's works continued to be subject to censorship, which prompted him to write *Die Zensur* (1908), a critique of German censoring practices. With marital issues by this time prominent in his personal life, in 1909–10 Wedekind wrote *Schloss Wetterstein* (*Castle Wetterstein*), a satirical treatment of marriage and of the bourgeois nuclear family; at the play's center is a rebellious teenage girl who turns to prostitution after her upbringing in an unstable household. As Wedekind explained in a letter to Georg Brandes (included in the "In Context" materials), the play comprises "three single act plays" that together form one drama. The three acts are closely interconnected in some respects, but divergent in others; notably, the third act alternates between verse and prose. The play was published in 1912, but a performance ban was put into effect immediately; it continued until after Wedekind's death.

In 1918 Wedekind underwent an appendectomy, after which he returned to the stage almost immediately and developed a hernia. His doctor was reluctant to operate, but Wedekind insisted on immediate surgery. He died from complications shortly thereafter, aged fifty three.

Cover of Castle Wettterstein, first edition

CASTLE WETTERSTEIN

Dedicated to
Kurt Martens
author of "Caritas Mimi"

[*Author's Preface*][1]

The play *Castle Wetterstein* contains my views about the inner needs that are the foundation of marriage and family. Thus, the dramatic material, the events, and the progress of the plot are of purely secondary importance. Their improbability was necessary because I needed wide spaces and freedom of movement to make room for my ideas. More importantly, I required dramatic intensity and effective staging. I would request, with all due respect, that critics refrain from forming a judgment about this play's qualities or deficiencies until they can base their views on an actual production. If this work is censored, that would not surprise me, since it would be nothing more than a logically necessary outcome of the notorious indifference and stupidity characteristic of our entire public life.

1 [*Author's Preface*] The author's preface is not preceded by a heading in the German text. Kurt Martens (1870–1945), to whom the work is dedicated, was a German writer, who, like Wedekind, spoke out against censorship in Germany.

Castle Wetterstein

DRAMATIS PERSONAE

Rüdiger, Baron Wetterstein
Leonore von Gystrow
Effie, her daughter
Meinrad Luckner
Karl Salzmann
Professor Dr. Scharlach[1]
Waldemar Uhlhorst
Matthias Taubert
Schigabet
Heiri Wipf
Chagnaral Tschamper of Atakama
Van Zeeter, hotel manager
Duvoisin, a police inspector
Housemaid
Waiter
Two policemen

ACT I

SCENE I[2]

(*Leonore, thirty-two years old, lies asleep on the sofa. She wakes up, yawns, rubs her eyes, and sits up.*)

LEONORE. What novel have I been reading? … "European Slave Life"[3] … (*Sitting up straight on the sofa.*) … and I dreamed of him again … Once I've drunk my tea, I won't need to think

---

1 *Professor Dr. Scharlach* "Scharlach" is also the German name for the illness scarlet fever.

2 *Act I Scene I* Wedekind's text does not specify the location or the date of the action; however, one or two lines in the play suggest that the plot begins in the 1880s (see footnotes for details). This scene seems to take place in Germany, probably Berlin.

3 *European Slave Life* Three-volume novel by prolific and popular German writer Friedrich Hackländer (1816–77), written in a comic style often compared at the time to that of Charles Dickens.

about him anymore. (*She stands up and rings a bell.*) Then I'll once again be sure how I'm supposed to deal with my dream life.

(*A Housemaid enters.*)

HOUSEMAID. Madam Major rang?
LEONORE. The tea.

(*The Housemaid exits.*)

LEONORE. God knows, it seems to me he can't get along without me either, even now.

(*Effie, fifteen years old, enters.*)

EFFIE. You've called for tea, Mother. Did you sleep well?
LEONORE. Who's been telling you I was asleep?
EFFIE. I didn't mean to upset you. Most people sleep in the afternoon. Tell me, Mother dear, would you allow me to go to the theater next Sunday with Gertrude Rickenbach?
LEONORE. You're talking to me, my child, as if you and I were complete strangers.
EFFIE. Yes, possibly. The most important thing for me in the next few years is not to be a stranger to myself.
LEONORE. I don't understand what you mean by that.
EFFIE. Well, right now there is nothing more important for me than to make a good marriage.
LEONORE. That's obviously true, my child. And for you, I hope, that can be done without too much trouble.
EFFIE. Don't concern yourself at all about it, Mother. I think of nothing else day and night. Here's the tea.

(*The Housemaid brings in the tea and exits.*)

LEONORE. (*Pouring the tea.*) For a woman everything always depends upon not demeaning herself by her marriage. A woman who feels unhappy in her marriage always has only herself to blame.
EFFIE. So why won't you allow me to go to the theater on Sunday?
LEONORE. Effie, I'm dumbfounded. Have you completely forgotten your father already?

EFFIE. If I don't go to the theater on Sunday, that won't bring Father back to us.

LEONORE. This incredible silliness of yours involves you a lot more than when you honor your father. The respect people pay you will never be greater than the honor you show your father. You will be called your father's child. What could be better than that?

EFFIE. Half of me is. The other half of me is the child of my mother.

LEONORE. That's not going to impress anyone.

EFFIE. To tell the truth, I don't think I suffer from pride or conceit, but if I'm anything at all, then I am at least one thing thanks to you, Mother dear, and that's a good match.

LEONORE. For us women that is something to consider only as advertizing, nothing more. A prudent woman would rather watch all her possessions being squandered in cold blood than ever claim them as her personal assets.

EFFIE. (*Blithely.*) Then, dear Mother, it's all the more necessary for us to perfect our feminine virtues and capabilities as early as possible.

LEONORE. I completely agree with you. We women cannot value our feminine assets highly enough.

EFFIE. Then why shouldn't I go to the theater next Sunday?

LEONORE. How can you ask me something like that? We're in mourning!

EFFIE. It will soon be a year and half!

LEONORE. Quite apart from the fact that you could be seen by someone in the theater. So long as you're my daughter, I will simply not tolerate how you so lightheartedly overlook your father's death.

EFFIE. (*After a pause.*) You do realize, Mother, that Gertrude von Rickenbach is appearing on stage in person.

LEONORE. I heard about it. As far as she's concerned, it's the best thing she can do. Her father squanders everything, and her mother's conduct cuts her out completely from marrying someone in her own class.

EFFIE. But suppose I get it into my head to shake off all concerns for our class with one energetic shrug of my shoulders, completely forget about getting married to someone in our circle, and simply go on the stage myself?

LEONORE. (*Simply and easily.*) I'd be sorry, Effie, but then you would no longer be my daughter.

EFFIE. Of course, you're totally convinced that I lack the slightest talent as an actress?

LEONORE. Why on earth should I think that? That's completely foolish. First, we women are by nature born actresses, because a woman who does not pretend cannot make any man happy. Second, you come from a noble family. You already have in your flesh and blood the vast majority of those talents people admire as theatrical art in the poor creatures who earn a living in the theater. But let me mention one point, Effie: Anyone who allows herself to be shown off in public for money does not belong in society. I will certainly not deny that there may well be women in theater who do nothing wrong. But gentlemen I know tell me these women are exceptions. In theater, for reasons having to do with business, everything is always purposefully designed as if all the audience members are just as disgraceful and warped as the people putting on the production.

EFFIE. I have always been entirely convinced that a theater show must be much more enjoyable for those putting it on than for those watching it.

LEONORE. That's exactly what's so undignified about it. Acting is a profession in which people get paid to enjoy themselves. No decent person does that.

EFFIE. But doesn't a woman also do that when she gets married?

LEONORE. I don't understand what you mean.

EFFIE. What I mean is that by marrying she lets herself get paid for her own pleasure.

LEONORE. She lets herself get paid? By whom?

EFFIE. By her husband, naturally. Who else?

LEONORE. God forbid! What are you thinking! In a marriage, the woman does not let herself get paid for her pleasures any more than her husband does. They both do what they do for each other for nothing.

EFFIE. That's strange. I'd always imagined it as entirely different.

LEONORE. You are obviously confusing two activities which have nothing whatsoever to do with one another. In my parents' house in Hamburg we had visits from actors. It's true. But they were merely tolerated. They were there on sufferance. Naturally, in exchange for that they had to provide the required entertainment. But people did not let them get closer than was socially unavoidable and necessary. What play is being produced on Sunday?

EFFIE. "The Wild Duck."

LEONORE. I don't know it. I've never heard of it.

EFFIE. It's by Ibsen.[1]

LEONORE. Good heavens! Isn't he the northern barbarian[2] who's been dragging marriage and the family through the mud and saying that all decent people are insane?

EFFIE. My dear Mother, you don't have the slightest idea how uneducated you are! Ibsen is in fashion!

LEONORE. Really?

EFFIE. The court goes to the theater when Ibsen is playing. The only reason you don't like Ibsen is that Father always criticized him in such a snide way. But I'm firmly convinced that nowadays Father would speak about him quite differently.

LEONORE. Really? Are you sure of that?

EFFIE. Today Father would say: Ibsen! My word, what a splendid fellow!

LEONORE. All right, Effie, tell me this: What does he really write about? Can you explain it to me in a few words?

EFFIE. He always writes more or less about what we ourselves have lived through.

LEONORE. You mean what he's lived through?

EFFIE. No, what we've lived through! We! You and I sitting here!

LEONORE. How does he know about that?

EFFIE. God knows. I didn't tell him anything!

---

1 *Ibsen* Norwegian Modernist playwright Henrik Ibsen (1828–1906), many of whose works were controversial for their criticisms of conventional social structures. *The Wild Duck* was first published in 1884.

2 *northern barbarian* Here Leonore uses the word *Kamtschadale* to describe Ibsen. The word *Kamtschadale* translates into English as *Kamchatkan*, denoting an original native inhabitant of the Kamchatka peninsula in Russia.

LEONORE. But then he can't be dragging family life through the mud, can he?

EFFIE. (*Cautiously.*) Well, Father was unfaithful to you, after all...

LEONORE. (*Straightening up indignantly.*) How dare you, child! What a thing to say!

EFFIE. (*Smiling.*) How dare I, dear Mother? I dare answer your question as politely as a young girl possibly can.

LEONORE. Be quiet, I tell you! No young girl speaks the way you did just now!

EFFIE. (*With a gentle smile.*) I can't let anyone doubt that I'm still a young girl, Mother dear, if I'm to marry a man from our social circles. Least of all you, because, of course, everyone says that you are best-placed to know all there is to know about me. In fact, I am a young girl. Or has anyone told you something else about me?

LEONORE. No. So far as I know, no one is spreading any gossip about you.

EFFIE. Well, God knows, I don't take any pride in that. But for me the most important task by far in my life now is to be a young girl. That's why I surely have a certain right to speak up for myself.

LEONORE. That may be so, but you have all the more reason to honor the memory of your father and not to keep insulting him in his grave.

EFFIE. (*Smiling.*) Mother, do you really think what I said is such a terrible insult to him?

LEONORE. You are inhuman! I beg you, Effie, never speak to me anymore in my lifetime about this disgrace! Since the days of our marriage your father's life was honorable. That was my pride—it meant everything to me! Or ... or ...

EFFIE. Or?

LEONORE. That's something the human mind simply cannot grasp! Or he must have been cheating on me from the first day we met! No! No! No! I have forgiven him, because I understood him inside and out. And because I understood myself. This trust I had in him and in myself—I will not let any power in heaven and earth rob me of that now that he is dead.

EFFIE. (*Stands up, embraces Leonore, and kisses her.*) You are so amazingly beautiful, Mother, when you get upset about Father. All the love I feel for you will not get me to ask you to forgive me.

LEONORE. (*Dabbing her eyes with a handkerchief.*) I can't describe how much you've hurt me with your heartless cruelty!

EFFIE. Don't be angry with me anymore, Mother. In that finishing school in Lausanne[1] with Madam Duplan, no one uttered a single word about when women are to be blocks of wood and when they are to be delicate flowers. But trust me, Mother, I'll learn soon enough.

LEONORE. Leave me alone, my child. I feel like a fish on dry sand. My feelings are overwhelming me from every side.

EFFIE. May I kiss your hand, Mother?

LEONORE. Kiss me on the mouth!

(*Effie gives her mother a quick kiss on the mouth.*)

LEONORE. (*Drawing back.*) Child!

EFFIE. What is it, Mother?

LEONORE. You must get married as soon as possible.

EFFIE. (*Cheerfully.*) I'll be able to manage that perfectly. Cheer up, Mother. I may really surprise you even yet.

(*Effie exits.*)

LEONORE. (*With a sigh.*) Thank God! I know I've been irritable with you. (*She takes the open book from the sofa.*) "European Slave Life." So who wrote this? (*She turns to the title page.*) Hackländer! Perhaps I'd prefer to read Ibsen next. With any luck he understands how to interpret dreams. (*She lies on the sofa and reads. There is a knock on the door.*) Come in!

---

1 *finishing school* School to which girls were sent to be educated in the finer points of etiquette, in preparation for entry into fashionable society; *Lausanne* City in the French-speaking region of Switzerland. Switzerland was well-known for its finishing schools, two of which were located in Lausanne.

Scene 2

(The Housemaid enters silently with a silver tray and brings a calling card to Leonore.)

LEONORE. *(Reading the card.)* Doctor Thilo von Chrysander—Court Chaplain retired—Consistorial Councillor[1]—*(To the* HOUSEMAID.) A moment! *(She sits down in front of a mirror, carefully arranges her hair, and then gets up.)* I'll see him now.

(The Housemaid leaves. Rüdiger enters quickly. He is twenty-seven years old and dressed in elegant formal clothes. Leonore threatens to lose her composure.)

RÜDIGER. Stay calm. You can trust your eyes. I am not a double of myself. I am me. No fainting, all right? Prove to me now that my unshakeable trust in your indomitable strength is not misplaced!

LEONORE. *(Struggling with all her strength to regain her composure.)* God ... my God ... how am I to survive this?

RÜDIGER. So you are not going to throw me out? *(Leonore stares at him without moving.)* Think about it! You are not throwing me out?

LEONORE. I ... words fail me ...

RÜDIGER. It would take only one word from you! *(Leonore does not answer.)* My thanks for that are infinite—like your magnanimity. *(Speaking very cautiously.)* Now I'm asking you to listen to me for a moment.

LEONORE. *(Collecting herself.)* You find yourself ... naturally ... in some sort of ... difficulty. You need my ... help ...

RÜDIGER. Yes, very much so.

LEONORE. Talk.

RÜDIGER. Wouldn't you like to sit?

LEONORE. That will not be necessary.

RÜDIGER. All right. We'll be sitting down soon enough.

LEONORE. Please get to the point.

---

1 *Consistorial Councillor* Clerical member of the consistory (i.e., a member of the administrative authority of the Protestant church).

RÜDIGER. I have come just as I am now straight from the fortress. You know that I was punished with a six-month sentence. If the military court had not been an empty formality, they would have had to sentence me to life in prison.

LEONORE. Why are you saying this to me? To me? You, the murderer of my husband, you presume too much … Perhaps you are afraid that my despair might not have been sufficiently heartbreaking?

RÜDIGER. I am afraid of something more serious. I fear you are committing an injustice against the deceased.

LEONORE. You, the man who murdered him, are afraid that I, his poor wife, am being unjust to him? Do not imagine I'll put up with your inhuman mockery a moment longer!

RÜDIGER. If the memory of your husband is dear to you, and your outrage convinces me it is, then you will thank me from the very bottom of your heart for being so extraordinarily bold.

LEONORE. Thank you? Me?! Does the most brutal feeling not tell you what … what a monster you are in my eyes? I loved my husband! You probably have no idea what that means. It is impossible for me to forget how much cheerfulness, strength, and patience I have sacrificed. Not that I am complaining. Heaven forbid! What was I until he finally made a woman out of me, one worthy of his love. Then I found my happiness in his happiness. What pleased him kindled my enthusiasm. What pained him I would have obliterated from the face of the earth without thinking about it. And I loved with such fire and hated so implacably that I thought of myself as the most heroic woman who had ever lived. And now the man who murdered him is saying I'm being unjust to the deceased.

RÜDIGER. Of course you are unjust to the Major if you honor in him nothing more noble than those merits which every wife has to see in her husband, if she is not going to start looking around for another man.

LEONORE. How dare you make that claim about me! Do you imagine I could have made do with an ordinary man?! God knows, there were enough men who desired me! But when I think back on them, merciful God, what shoddy goods they were in comparison with him. The infinite depth of his heart was something I had never anticipated, something an ordinary man simply cannot imagine. And his nobility! His inexhaustible generosity to me! And all his life he was the most competent in every field. The best horseman! The most charming companion! If people talked of military service or campaigns, I never saw anyone whose argument prevailed against his.

RÜDIGER. When his wife is present, that is surely obvious!

LEONORE. You attribute these virtues to me?! If so, you are simply demonstrating you had no idea of the stature of the man you killed!

RÜDIGER. Now you are offering proof that you are wronging him.

LEONORE. (*After recovering from her amazement.*) You are displaying an unmatched insolence.

RÜDIGER. Should I consider Major Gystrow especially honorable because his own wife considers him the most marvelous man who ever lived?

LEONORE. What you say seems to me like the words of a mental patient.

RÜDIGER. I can see no higher value in that than I could if he had wanted to think it particularly virtuous of you that no other woman had loved him more devotedly that you did.

LEONORE. (*Rigid with astonishment.*) What finer thing can you say about a married woman than that she loves her husband above everything else?

RÜDIGER. That's nothing but natural history. I could, for example, say about her that she is the epitome of youthful freshness. That she has an intelligent mind which, if she can freely develop it, would think nothing sacred other than crystal clear, inexorable reason. I could say of her that her powers of perception work with an agility which is rarely encountered, even among men. But, above all, I can say of her that such a tempestuous passion lies chained up inside her that from childhood on she has only dreamt with divine trembling of the moment when she can see her ridiculously small ego and its domestic miseries sink once and for all deep into the abyss beneath her.

LEONORE. And would you let yourself be seduced by such sinister devilish tricks into the clutches of such a weird person?

You, a man who claims to have high expectations? All those things you find so admirable in this paragon—those are the very things you could not fight ruthlessly enough, if your life were not to become a living hell! Other than our birth and our death, marriage is the most inexorable thing we creatures are subjected to. If you consider yourself an exception, then you'll have to pay for that in your marriage with extreme disagreements and humiliations.

RÜDIGER. (*Smiling.*) You have no idea how comical your fears sound to me. If I feel myself demeaned I need only turn my back. Then I'll find the highest esteem I could wish for. By the way, I completely forgot to tell you one of the most beautiful qualities of my chosen one.

LEONORE. Then say it! What are you waiting for?

RÜDIGER. The woman I adore would go to her death for the man she loves.

LEONORE. If you love your own life, then guard yourself against such a woman. A woman who would go to her death for her husband would also go after him with a bullet through the chest, the moment she felt he had insulted her!

RÜDIGER. Then why didn't you shoot the Major?

LEONORE. Why did I not murder my husband? You can ask that?

RÜDIGER. But he insulted you!

LEONORE. Because I loved him! Who does the slightest harm to a person he loves? But even if I had wanted to kill him ten times over, he was cold and stiff by the time I received the report of his misconduct. You were too quick for me, forcing him in that treacherous way to face your dreadful murder weapon.

RÜDIGER. Out of respect for the Major, I must stipulate that the bullet from a soldier is at least as deadly as one from a—reservist.[1]

LEONORE. (*Getting angry.*) Do not make jokes about his fate in this house! I am the guardian of his memory, and I will not permit it! A man like you should never challenge anyone to a duel with pistols. You, a man who is known as someone who

1 *reservist* Member of a military reserve force, which may be called to duty when needed.

once earned his living with public displays of his skill shooting a revolver!

RÜDIGER. For me this moment is too sacred to spend defending myself against groundless suspicions printed in the newspapers. If the rumor you mention had been confirmed, I would not have been condemned to the fortress but to prison, perhaps even to the penitentiary. Of course, you know as well as I do that I was not free to make any sort of choice. If I had not challenged the Major, then today I would be a man without honor.

LEONORE. What do I care about your honor!

RÜDIGER. But I care about it! For example, I could not possibly have faced you like this at all.

LEONORE. Could not possibly … face me … What gives you the slightest justification to do this? In spite of everything I still find that incomprehensible.

RÜDIGER. We are partners in suffering! Thanks to your husband I have lost my woman.

LEONORE. You mean your wife? I congratulate you on your loss! Your wife threw herself at my husband's feet like a wild creature that could no longer find mercy in any human soul! On the evening of that winter day my husband was buried, I found letters from your wife in which she signed herself "Your slave." What do you have to mourn in a wife who exposes a man like you to ridicule, in order to destroy the happiness of another woman who during her life has never harmed her in the slightest?

RÜDIGER. I was legally divorced from her four weeks ago. Both my children were, of course, put into my custody. I have just handed them over to my wife's mother for her to raise.

LEONORE. And what will become of her now?

RÜDIGER. Of whom?

LEONORE. Of the most unfortunate creature on God's earth! How miserable things must now look inside this wretched soul! Everything, even the last most pitiful happiness, gambled away! But such changelings[1] deserve nothing better than to

---

1 *changeling* Newborn child substituted for another without the parents' knowledge; more broadly, changeable or fickle person, traitor.

be destroyed. Life would be blissful happiness without limit, if these dismal mischief makers did not spread their poison from below!

RÜDIGER. My divorced wife was not that degenerate. She did not give herself away out of mindless frivolity. She let herself be seduced by her ill-advised malice. She believed I had cheated on her, because someone had falsely told her I was behaving suspiciously.

LEONORE. She was told you were acting suspiciously? What does that mean?

RÜDIGER. Someone wrote her anonymous letters in which he told her that in the evenings I spent with my friends I was visiting a dancer from the Olympia Theater.[1]

LEONORE. And on the basis of this hocus pocus, my husband is supposed to have let himself be ensnared by this person as a substitute?! As a substitute! You dare say that to my face?!

RÜDIGER. I am very sorry about it, Madam, but you are still being unjust to the Major.

LEONORE. Are you going to make some sort of claim that he would have had to wait until your wife was desperate if he ever had a mind to spend time with other women?

RÜDIGER. All his life the Major could have had any woman he wanted. That's obvious. But since he was your husband, he would have only experienced the most pathetic disappointment every time. What he found interesting about my former wife was the similarity between his heartfelt sadness and hers. He was looking for consolation.

LEONORE. Why consolation, if he felt so happy with me?!

RÜDIGER. Someone made him suspect you.

LEONORE. Suspect me?

RÜDIGER. Someone wrote letters to him containing undeniable proof that you were being unfaithful to him.

LEONORE. Me?! That I was being … ?! Almighty God! And he believed that?!

---

1 *Olympia Theater* Probably referring to the Olympia Theater in Paris, a large music hall that opened in 1888 with the famous French can-can dancer known as "La Goulue" as the headliner.

RÜDIGER. He was an honest man. He did not overestimate his own qualities.

LEONORE. (*Crying out.*) No, no! That's impossible! He cannot have doubted me for a moment!

RÜDIGER. He had doubts, and they made him desperate.

LEONORE. He cannot have had doubts! That's unreasonable! No, no! Now he can no longer speak for himself, I will not permit any living person to try to convince me of it.

RÜDIGER. In an emergency, reason is always the first comrade to cut and run. If he had thought about these suspicions dispassionately, he would just as dispassionately have set about investigating them. Then it would have been extremely easy for him to realize they were false. But his love for you made it completely impossible for him to put any faith in the insinuations even for an instant. All that was left for him was the immense pain of seeing his life's happiness destroyed.

LEONORE. But am I a block of wood? In those last weeks before that New Year's morning I lived by his side in unsuspecting happiness. How could I not have felt the slightest sign of his distrust and his confusion, of all his harrowing ordeal?

RÜDIGER. He was a soldier. He controlled himself. The least sign of his torment would have led to a quarrel with you, and he lacked the courage necessary for that. In the meantime, the agonizing pretense in his own house drove him to the house of my former wife, where he found a woman with the most candid and honest understanding of his situation.

LEONORE. (*Wringing her hands.*) So that was it! It's true! Something as horrible as this has never happened before! He could not believe for a minute that I ... that I would hurt him in the slightest! And with this image in his mind he entered the fight and stood face to face with death! It's simply unimaginable how appalling his despair must have been. With a curse against me he took up his weapon. With a curse against me he sank to his knees. Then he was not even murdered—he was seeking death! And I'm his murderer! What in the world did people tell him about me?

RÜDIGER. How should I know that?

LEONORE. (*Crying out.*) You know! I see it in your face! Tell me!

RÜDIGER. You cannot listen to that now.

LEONORE. Haven't I already heard the worst? Do you mean to keep me like this, still stretched out on the rack?[1] What did people tell him about me?

RÜDIGER. It is too absurd for you to listen to at such a serious moment.

LEONORE. So you do know?

RÜDIGER. Yes.

LEONORE. Almighty God, how do you know all these terrible details?

RÜDIGER. From the sessions of the military court, which took place behind closed doors. They naturally took extreme care to hide these unpleasant facts from you.

LEONORE. Then the tribunal was a dishonest pretense! Why was I not summoned to appear?

RÜDIGER. Your innocence was completely beyond doubt.

LEONORE. But did the proceedings not establish who wrote the letters that destroyed two unsuspecting families?

RÜDIGER. No, they did not discover that. But I came here to reveal that to you.

LEONORE. (*Apprehensively.*) Stop talking! I implore you by Almighty God. Do not say another word! I am not strong enough to listen to such appalling details.

RÜDIGER. I was the one who wrote the letters.

LEONORE. (*Crying out.*) No, no—that's not true!

RÜDIGER. Do I appear to you incapable of such a thing?

LEONORE. (*Wide-eyed, staring at him.*) No! You were capable of it!

RÜDIGER. And now I'm asking you to become my wife.

LEONORE. I ... saw that ... coming.

RÜDIGER. For five full years, day after day, night after night, in my heart I have dreamed of no other goal. When I met you five years ago, at first sight I had the unshakeable conviction I could not find a person with a soul as passionate and great as yours a second time in this life. One victory today has already validated my conviction. You are indeed the wife I have been fighting for in the past five years. Now I am no longer afraid to

1 *rack* Torture instrument upon which one's body is tied and then stretched.

take responsibility for my actions. The victims have not fallen in vain.

LEONORE. Leave my house.

RÜDIGER. What is the point of that now? You underestimate the significance of this moment. You underestimate the power you have in your hands. One word from you will be enough to send me to the penitentiary.

LEONORE. Is that true? Do you swear that's true? Or are you trying to win my confidence with this pretence?

RÜDIGER. Whether that is true or not, either way your duty is now clear beyond a doubt. As the wife of the dead man, you have an obligatory and sacred duty to declare in public everything you have found out.

LEONORE. And then?

RÜDIGER. Then I will surrender to my fate. Why not?

LEONORE. (*With an enormous effort to control herself.*) Go! Leave here! I do not know you! I have not understood a single word you've been saying. Do you want me to call for help?

RÜDIGER. Your tone is not genuine. Why not simply ring the bell?

LEONORE. In any case, I don't understand why the noise we've been making hasn't disturbed anyone.

RÜDIGER. Now you simply need to make a choice between fulfilling your most sacred duty—denouncing me—and the decision to become my wife. Please make up your mind.

LEONORE. Your words are nothing more than the most horrible braggadocio.[1] I am not going to be browbeaten by monstrous apparitions. I don't see the slightest compelling reason why I should choose between two fires of hell.

RÜDIGER. I assure you there is no third option available to you. As strong as you may be, you will not be able to keep my secret. You will hint at something, and your sister-in-law or someone else will burn with curiosity. You will be given no peace. You will feel relieved of a hellish burden, and I—I will be regretting my stupidity.

LEONORE. You are right! You are perfectly right! No one can keep silent about something so monstrous!

---

1 *braggadocio* Boasting.

RÜDIGER. No one except my wife! For five years you've been my accomplice.

LEONORE. I keep hoping that this business of accusing yourself comes down to some sort of blackmail.

RÜDIGER. To the greatest thing you have to give!

LEONORE. Then finally, for God's sake, state a specific amount!

RÜDIGER. You know I want you to be my wife.

LEONORE. Yes, yes. Of course, you want that, don't you? That way the amount of money will end up being as large as possible! I will purchase my freedom from you. I offer you … fifty thousand marks![1]

RÜDIGER. That's too little.

LEONORE. Fifty-five thousand …

RÜDIGER. Those are just empty words.

LEONORE. I have more than that.

RÜDIGER. You cannot possibly give away ten per cent of your entire wealth.

LEONORE. What will it take for you to settle?

RÜDIGER. What I want is for you to become my wife.

LEONORE. I should marry the murderer of my husband?

RÜDIGER. The man who up to this point has made the greatest sacrifice for you.

LEONORE. That would be a torture chamber of a marriage!

RÜDIGER. There's no such thing as a torture chamber of a marriage. People either love each other, or they separate! Most healthy people become happy couples. Why shouldn't we become a happy couple? Marriage is not being bound up in chains, except for those mental cripples who think that's what it means. If I cannot adore my wife, then someone should steal her from me.

LEONORE. Almighty Heaven! The chivalry of a horse trader! And I am to belong to you on the basis of this confession?

RÜDIGER. You are not to belong to me! You belong to yourself! Marriage is there for people, not people for marriage! Your

---

1 *marks* Until the introduction of the euro in 2002, the mark was the unit of German currency.

happiness, your free development—those are the most sacred goals of our life together.

LEONORE. That is admittedly a new goal for me! A surprising goal! But you! To whom do you belong then! Don't you belong to me?

RÜDIGER. To far greater degree, at least, than you belong to me. Have you forgotten that already?

LEONORE. If only that is true! I ask myself that over and over again. Or are you boasting of vile acts other people have committed?

RÜDIGER. Now you need only ask me whether I want you for my wife because of your possessions!

LEONORE. (*Quickly.*) God forbid! No, no, I have no desire to offend you. That is completely beyond me. But what if after our wedding it turns out that you were nothing but a husband who had been betrayed ... ?

RÜDIGER. Permit me, madam, to be on my way.

LEONORE. You've forgotten where you're going!

RÜDIGER. What concern is that of yours?

LEONORE. Stay here!

RÜDIGER. Only if you give me a down payment!

LEONORE. What does that mean?

RÜDIGER. A guaranteed pledge.

LEONORE. What are you demanding?

RÜDIGER. If I have to ask for it first, then there's not much for me to win here.

LEONORE. Then help yourself.

RÜDIGER. (*Turning towards the door.*) I will not force myself on anyone!

LEONORE. (*Runs to him and throws her arms around his neck.*) Here I am! Here I am!

RÜDIGER. (*Kissing her.*) I'm holding in my arms the prize for victory in the five-year struggle!

LEONORE. Aren't you afraid of a woman who lets herself be kissed by the murderer of her husband?

RÜDIGER. (*Smiling.*) Perhaps I should be feared less than you? We are a match for one another. Neither one of us has an advantage over the other.

LEONORE. What if you now come across a woman in whom you find all the charm and attractive qualities you have always valued in women. Will you then betray me with her?

RÜDIGER. No, no, my child. You need not expect such foolishness from me.

LEONORE. Why is that foolish? When I asked my first husband about that, he shrugged his shoulders and let me know that the truth of the matter was he would be prepared to do that at any moment. I always used to quietly give thanks to Heaven that in reality things had not yet come to that. And, God knows, even now I'd still stake my life on it, the lapse which cost him his life was his first and only lapse during our marriage.

RÜDIGER. Of that I'm absolutely certain.

LEONORE. So after our first kiss, you look me right in the eye and tell me with an impartiality people only use when they are speaking of historical facts that you will never betray me?!

RÜDIGER. If I betray my wife, then I have a wife who lets herself be betrayed. Joking about the experience does not help. If my wife allows me—whom she counts upon for her happiness—to betray her, then she will inevitably be betrayed in the same way by all the rest of the world. That market woman who sells her a partridge will betray her. Who has the partridge served to him? Who has to struggle to force the partridge down? Who has to pay for the partridge?

LEONORE. Excellent! Now can you also tell me what emerges from this chain of reasoning if you turn it around? If I betray you ... ?

RÜDIGER. What's sauce for the goose is sauce for the gander! If you betray me, then you have definitely married a man who allows himself to be betrayed. And by a woman, too. My business friends will not need to be told twice. They will look on you as an illuminating example. In a very short time I'll have been cheated of the last shirt on my back, and if you do not wish to become a beggar, you'll have every reason to look around you as quickly as you can for another partner in life.

LEONORE. (*Clapping her hands.*) Bravo! You are the first person on God's earth from whom I have heard a truly human word about these highly dangerous matters. (*She kisses him.*) You are a jack-of-all-trades! In our circles when these questions arise all we hear are either dirty stories or biblical quotations.

RÜDIGER. Human feelings speak an infernally thievish jargon. Whoever trusts their gibberish is sold off and betrayed.

LEONORE. So do you really think the wife has just as much right to be unfaithful as the husband?

RÜDIGER. That's not my view of it at all. I simply believe that the wife has as much right to be unfaithful as her husband's lover does. It's self-evident that the husband has an unimaginably greater right to be unfaithful than the wife! That's an irrefutable fact! But there are no circumstances in which he has a greater right to be unfaithful than his wife's lover has.

LEONORE. That is an amazing revelation! Never in my life would I have imagined that the world was arranged in a way so easy to understand! Where do you get all these pearls of wisdom?

RÜDIGER. From my experience. I have always found that mutual infidelity, when both parties are completely honest, leads to the most pleasant and comfortable parting of the ways. But in the process both of them, of course, lose all the fruits of their earlier efforts. They tear open one hole in order to fill in another.

LEONORE. What do you mean?

RÜDIGER. Each of them shrugs off one burden in order to take on another.

LEONORE. Ah, I see!

RÜDIGER. What do you think I meant?

LEONORE. I thought you were speaking personally.

RÜDIGER. You can construe my words however you like. The main thing is that they're still true!

LEONORE. (*She embraces and kisses him.*) Marvelous! Marvelous! Marvelous!—Whoever can speak like that is allowed everything, is forgiven everything!

RÜDIGER. Be mine!

LEONORE. Take me! (*A prolonged ringing sounds from the hall.*) What's that? Who's ringing the bell so rudely?

RÜDIGER. Are we the only ones at home?

LEONORE. (*Smiling.*) The Major!

RÜDIGER. I tell you, you are doing him an injustice.

LEONORE. Me? How?

RÜDIGER. We should leave him to rest in peace!

LEONORE. (*Listening.*) I think the girl has gone to open the door.

RÜDIGER. After all, he has not harmed us.

LEONORE. All of a sudden, I feel so strange here, as if the entire house was falling apart.

SCENE 3

(*Effie, wearing a hat and coat, enters quickly, runs to her mother, and flings her arms around her mother's neck.*)

EFFIE. Mother, Mother, I've become engaged!

LEONORE. You, as well! But you're still much too young for that!

EFFIE. But you told me I had to get married as quickly as I could … (*Noticing Rüdiger.*) … O my God! A ghost! On the day of my engagement!

LEONORE. (*Introducing Rüdiger.*) Rüdiger von Wetterstein, my husband-to-be.

RÜDIGER. There is not the slightest reason, my dear young lady, for you to draw back from me. Until you are married, the engagement between your mother and me will obviously remain a secret.

EFFIE. Mother, Mother?—I don't know—Am I still alive?—Or am I dreaming?

LEONORE. That is how all fifteen-year-old girls feel.

EFFIE. Is that true, Mother?

RÜDIGER. Since you are engaged to be married yourself, you would have soon been separated from your mother anyway.

LEONORE. Who are you engaged to?

EFFIE. I can't bring myself to say it …

RÜDIGER. You can be certain, my dear young lady, that I regret the death of your father as profoundly as if in his death I had killed my own father. But now, my dear young lady, after you have lost your father, do you wish to lose your mother, as well? If your mother does not like the man you have just this minute chosen, would that make you send him on his way? Can you expect your mother to banish the man she has chosen for herself for your sake?

EFFIE. (*Kissing her mother's hand.*) I wish you happiness, my dear Mother. I understand you. You cannot do otherwise. You must like him.

LEONORE. What about you, my child?

EFFIE. (*Joyfully.*) The handsomest man in the world!

RÜDIGER. Naturally, that is to be expected. And, more than that, he is also one of the richest.

LEONORE. (*To Effie.*) Really? Count D'Armont?

EFFIE. I met him down in the Platanenallee.[1] I asked him if he really thought the Pope would be coming to Berlin for the Crown Prince's accession to the throne. Then he said, "It is no longer possible for me to imagine I can endure this life without you." I was totally frank with him and said that to a certain extent, when all is said and done, it was a matter of complete indifference to me who I was married to. Only I could not guarantee that I was particularly well-suited to marriage at all. Then he asked me whether he could pay us a visit. "That's up to you," I said. If he does not come here by tomorrow noon, the fault will lie with the old Countess. She claims I'm a flirt.

RÜDIGER. I know their family doctor. He will have to send her away for a few weeks.

EFFIE. How will he manage that?

RÜDIGER. He'll convince her she has heart trouble. Then she'll move into a sanatorium.

EFFIE. You're a jack of all trades!

LEONORE. Effie!

EFFIE. What, Mother? I've often heard you use that expression.

LEONORE. Don't be angry with me over this, my child. But I must ask you to be a little more respectful.

---

1 *Platanenallee* The German *Platanenallee* means *avenue of sycamores* or *avenue of plane trees*, but *Platanenallee* is also the name of a street in Berlin, Tübingen, Bad Essen, and elsewhere. It is not clear here whether the word refers to the name of a specific street or is simply a descriptive term. Nor is it clear whether or not Leonore and Effie live in Berlin.

EFFIE. (*Kissing her mother.*) You are right, Mother. Of course, it's not all that easy, but I will try to say "Father." We women have to stick together.

RÜDIGER. Our emotional life consists of overestimating the value of human relationships. Everyone is replaceable.

ACT 2

SCENE I

(*A richly and elegantly furnished room in the Hotel Beaurivage in Ouchy on the shores of Lake Geneva. In the background there is an open balcony door with a view over the water. It is evening, and the lights are on.*)

LUCKNER. (*Walking around the room.*) That clean-living husband of yours, Rüdiger, Baron von Wetterstein, has, in the course of the past year, embezzled from me diamonds valued at two million. What a god-damned song and dance! (*He breaks out in booming laughter.*) Holy cannon fodder! If the baboon had at least buried the diamonds somewhere in the earth! He's been cramming the stones down the throat of every shady dealer in both hemispheres, like rotten bananas.

LEONORE. I find you truly irritating, but in precisely the opposite way you imagine. Do not assume you can look upon Rüdiger and me as your sacrificial victims.

LUCKNER. Almighty Panama Canal! (*He laughs.*) Take a leaf out of my book. The pleasure is costing me a cool two million. Great Brahmaputra![1] (*He laughs.*) Has Wetterstein never chanted our priceless Latin school song for you?

> Alas, the Maid got such a scare
> She could no longer perch up there.
> She clutched the stool with all her might,
> So she would not fall off in fright.

LEONORE. Thank God in Heaven! The monster is completely drunk, at least.

---

1 *Brahmaputra* River in China, India, and Bangladesh.

LUCKNER. Me ... drunk? (*He laughs.*) You really don't know me at all, do you? No, no, my heavenly sacrificial creature! Even if my father did found the most magnificent brewery company in the Rhineland-Palatinate[1] a thousand times over. But since my earliest youth I've been competing with our strongest brewery workers in lifting barrels full of beer. Doing that turns every muscle in one's entire body into bullet-proof armor plate.

LEONORE. Rüdiger has no idea of what was going on around him. Even now, Rüdiger doesn't have the slightest suspicion of what a monster he is dealing with in you.

LUCKNER. Ah well! The very first time we were together in the mines, you, him, and me, back then in Africa, I could have bullied the fellow out of all your shares in the wink of an eye. But you were standing at his side, gaping up at him like a tortoise at a telegraph pole. So I said to myself: one can only catch such splendid examples of womanhood through the men they love. And he stared at me like a bloated capitalist dismissing a newspaper boy. Heavens above! Great heavens above! Then I said to myself: No, Rüdiger von Wetterstein, we are not going to part from each other without a word or two. A woman like this, I told myself, is born only once in a hundred years. The man who does not take her where he finds her, even for two million ...

LEONORE. Are you going to let me speak sensibly to you for a moment?

LUCKNER. (*Smiling.*) You see, I am a man ... I am in fact a unique individual! An extraordinary person! For instance, I'd like you to feel, among other things, my head just this once. Posemuckel and Sumatra![2] Have you ever in your life seen such a gnarled lump on any human body?

---

1 *Rhineland-Palatinate* The German word *Rheinpfalz* (usually translated *Rhineland-Palatinate*) designates a specific part of Germany (now one of the sixteen German states in the Federal Republic), the area in western Germany bordering France, Belgium, and Luxembourg. Its capital is Mainz.

2 *Posemuckel and Sumatra!* An exclamation. Sumatra is a large island in Indonesia, while Posemuckel may refer to a village in Poland, though it is unclear what may be meant by the reference.

LEONORE. If Rüdiger remains co-owner of our mines in Jagersfontein,[1] as he has a perfect right to do, then in the course of the next five years he can replenish your diamonds for you right down to the tiniest stone.

LUCKNER. (*Breaks out in booming laughter.*) You see, just like me with my head! Because that's my weakest spot. A world-famous historical fact, respected by boxers and wrestlers all over the globe. Sailors and butcher's assistants who don't give a shit about the police and providence, any more than people like us do about an art gallery, when we fight each other never lay their tiniest finger on my head. Up here, you see, where my hair is most thickly curled, there you can knock me out with a wooden spoon, but other than that ... Holy Hailstones! ... And as for you! Brummfiedel, Pestilence and Armageddon! Your unfathomable emerald-green tiger's eyes! You're not letting them shine now because you're feeling spiteful. And then your hair! Holy Hound of Hades! Enough to break a man's heart on the spot! O you Bells of Hell! In my dreams I saw you rise up like a glowing cannon ball, hissing and spitting, and I was blown apart, scattered to the four winds. And your hand! Your hand! Sulphur Pools of Hell! Your hand!—And then your walk, Blood-rain and thunder! You see, Madam, from my youth on I've been a reliable judge of horseflesh. I'd look over a horse with the same eyes I'd use to choose my mistress. The most hidden flaw stares back at me magnified a million times. Ah yes, millions. If Wetterstein and I had not gone into the diamond washing[2] business, I'd have earned just as many millions as an American dealer in high-end horses.

LEONORE. (*Still in the chair, wringing her hands.*) Sacred God in Heaven, O God, show me how I can make this misbegotten monstrosity aware of how he repels and disgusts me!

LUCKNER. (*With a wicked laugh.*) O you sad, broken lily! You conceited little fool! Do you think I expect you to love me?! Holy

1 *Jagersfontein* Open-pit diamond mine in South Africa (now abandoned). Diamonds were discovered on the property in 1870, and the operation was officially closed in 1969.

2 *diamond washing* Process of washing dirt from diamonds and separating them from the rest of the rock aggregate, using a large but moveable machine.

Howitzers[1] on the Hilltops! Please just save your love for that sugary young man of yours. Almighty Paradise of Fools! There's nothing I find more excruciating than being personally attractive to a woman. My private concerns are none of her business.

LEONORE. In any case, I'd put a bullet through my head first.

LUCKNER. Then please hurry up and do it! Your husband, that thirty-carat rhinoceros, urgently needs someone finally to take him firmly in hand. After a five-year absence from the world he will be reborn. Once he's done his time, his new glory days will begin. In six months he'll be the first secretary and right hand of the director … (*Listening.*) God-fearing World Parliament, those are his footsteps!

SCENE 2

(*Rüdiger von Wetterstein enters in a hurry.*)

RÜDIGER. (*As soon as he sees Luckner.*) What are you doing here?

LUCKNER. We are lighting a cigarette, if you've no objection. (*He lights a cigarette.*)

RÜDIGER. Would you get out of here!

(*Rüdiger goes for Luckner's throat, intending to throw him through the door. The two men struggle. Luckner throws Rüdiger into an armchair and lights another cigarette.*)

LUCKNER. You diamond washerwoman! If only you had legs as strong as our arms! Heaven, Death, and Divorce Courts! (*He laughs.*) You had the heathenish madness to found the Wetterstein dynasty. Hammurabi, Caesar, Bonaparte,[2] Wetterstein! You incomparable ass, you would-be Napoleon, you idiot of the first water,[3] you wanted to be the fifth great man on this

1 *Howitzers* Types of cannons.

2 *Hammurabi, Caesar, Bonaparte* Luckner provides examples of three powerful dynastic leaders: Hammurabi (c. 1810 BCE–c. 1750 BCE), king of the First Babylonian Dynasty; Gaius Julius Caesar (100 BCE–44 BCE), dictator of the Roman Republic; and Napoléon Bonaparte (1769–1821), emperor of the French.

3 *of the first water* Phrase used in diamond mining to refer to first-rate diamonds, those which are unusually large, brilliant, and transparent.

earthly sphere—Rockefeller, Morgan, Krupp, Carnegie,[1] and Wetterstein! (*He laughs.*)

RÜDIGER. (*In the armchair.*) I find it impossible to sort out any ideas right now. Give me until tomorrow.

LUCKNER. Not even for Chicago! Or even if it rains cowshit! We've been waiting for two years. In half an hour we'll call it quits. It's all been so divinely arranged—words cannot describe it. When the woman fights back, then the man's power grows superhuman. The more desperate her resistance, the more skillfully the man sweeps it out of the way. But if the man resists ... well, enjoy your dinner!

LEONORE. (*Moving up close to Luckner with great determination.*) Aren't you afraid I could strangle you with these two hands?

LUCKNER. Not in the slightest! We'll be waiting in our sitting room. We'll stay at the hotel till ten o'clock.

(*Luckner exits.*)

SCENE 3

RÜDIGER. (*Getting up.*) I'm leaving you alone, Leonore. Luckner has informed the police. I do not wish to confront my fate here, in your presence.

LEONORE. Then I'll go with you.

RÜDIGER. In that case it makes no sense for me to leave. We might both just as well remain here.

LEONORE. Do you want to end your life?

RÜDIGER. No. I really wanted to, but I'm sure I lack the strength.

LEONORE. Surely there's only one appropriate course of action for both of us—to remove ourselves from the world?

RÜDIGER. Why? If I am no longer there, no one can harm you.

1 *Rockefeller, Morgan, Krupp, Carnegie* Four names associated with wealth, influence, and industry during the nineteenth century: John D. Rockefeller (1839–1937), American oil industry magnate; J.P. Morgan (1837–1913), American banker and business leader; the German Krupp family, who were known for their production of steel and ammunition; and Andrew Carnegie (1835–1919), Scottish-American magnate of the steel industry.

LEONORE. When you are no longer there? How does no one being able to harm me do me any good then?

RÜDIGER. You were happy before you met me. You'll find happiness again.

LEONORE. Those are just words. You don't even believe them yourself. I first learned what happiness is when I met you.

RÜDIGER. So much the worse for you. In my life I am always dissatisfied with myself. At my parents' house I was an unhappy child; in my first marriage I was an unhappy husband. I made you unspeakably miserable when I destroyed your happiness. And since we've lived together, I don't feel any happier than I did before.

LEONORE. (*Crying out in anguish.*) O! O! To have to hear that now!

RÜDIGER. Forgive me, forgive me. It's just that since I was born I've never been a consistent person. Since my childhood, two hostile races have been fighting a murderously destructive war inside me.

LEONORE. Right now your entire life seems dark and gloomy, just as in happy times you always see everything bathed in the most brilliant sunshine.

RÜDIGER. If only we two were not chained together!

LEONORE. How are we chained together? Come on, how?

RÜDIGER. How are we chained? How? Yes, yes, yes! I ask myself that all the time.

LEONORE. (*After a pause, with a groan.*) I think I know, Rüdiger, what it is that keeps the two of us welded to each other.

RÜDIGER. The criminal acts we carried out together. I chased your husband to get together with my wife and, once that happened, used it as an excuse for telling her to leave. Then I freed us from your husband by tricking him into a duel. Later we got married and wanted to create for ourselves a life whose splendor would justify the immense sacrifices it cost.

LEONORE. That is just morbid and effeminate wallowing in emotion, nothing but superstition—gloomy images you never even thought about when we were happy with our lives.

RÜDIGER. (*Groaning.*) Then tell me the name of the awful chain that will not let us separate from each other.

LEONORE. That's extremely easy. Whenever you wanted us to separate, I did everything I possibly could to prevent it. And when I wanted us to separate, you did everything you could to keep us together.

RÜDIGER. But why? Tell me, why did we do that? Why were we always so unreasonable?

LEONORE. I know as little about that as you do. But I do know one thing: exploring this riddle now is no help at all.

RÜDIGER. That's too bad! Unfortunately that's what we've told ourselves every time unhappiness has left our reason paralyzed.

LEONORE. You say it's unfortunate? I say, thank God! You have no answer? You are finding this a struggle? Rüdiger, we do not have much time left. Don't we want to end this quickly?

RÜDIGER. That's easy to say.

LEONORE. (*Quickly.*) It's over soon.

RÜDIGER. Here you go. (*He puts a revolver on the table.*) Now do it!

LEONORE. You don't know what to do next? (*Reaching for the weapon.*) I do!

RÜDIGER. (*Grabbing her arm and holding her hand back.*) Leonore! For God's sake!

LEONORE. Both of us have been demanding too much from the world if we lack the necessary courage now!

RÜDIGER. (*Frantic.*) I love you!

LEONORE. That's the first time I've heard you use that suspicious word.

RÜDIGER. Well, what do you think about both of us bringing things to an end?

LEONORE. I can't think about it. It's all over. From the first day of our marriage we were no longer a part of good society.

RÜDIGER. That was an unexpected setback for us. Good society is the society in which one does good business.

LEONORE. You stake your entire character on belonging in the big, wide world.

RÜDIGER. This rebuke comes late!

LEONORE. It's not a rebuke! No, Rüdiger! How could I do that?

RÜDIGER. The big, wide world is the world where one does great business.

LEONORE. Up to this point no one has threatened our very existence.

RÜDIGER. Except for us.

LEONORE. But why?

RÜDIGER. Why? Isn't that obvious to you? Because our human dignity is threatened!

LEONORE. Human dignity! That's nonsense! Is it dignified for a man to spend five years of his life as a hangman's slave?

RÜDIGER. A hangman's slave? So you are shifting the responsibility all onto me?

LEONORE. How did you arrive at that awful suspicion? Have you ever kept a secret from me?

RÜDIGER. You always knew as well as I did what I was doing. In his own era, Jesus Christ came up with a view of the world suitable for the army of outcasts that nowadays are sitting in the penitentiary or the lunatic asylum.

LEONORE. And what did he say about us women?

RÜDIGER. (*Crying out.*) Leonore! How can you ask that question? (*Calmer.*) Do as you wish! Then I'll do what I wish! Human dignity is not a monkey jacket.[1] No, human dignity is breath, nourishment, light. Human dignity grows out of the marriage of the parents and is the foundation for the marriages of the children.

LEONORE. (*Reaching for the revolver.*) Here is our human dignity!

RÜDIGER. Do you wish to kill me? (*He stands up and looks her in the eye.*) Try it, if you can!

LEONORE. If you don't want me to ...

RÜDIGER. Please do it! But quickly!

LEONORE. (*Pulls her hand back.*) Where am I supposed to get the strength for that!

RÜDIGER. Naturally I am once again the one at fault!

LEONORE. (*Rushing to hold him around the chest.*) No, no! I'm to blame! It's my fault!

---

1 *monkey jacket* Short, close-fitting coat worn by sailors, waiters, or military officers in their mess.

RÜDIGER. That's why Christianity conquered the world. People never really know whether they are back again in the penitentiary or the asylum.

LEONORE. And whoever feels he bears no blame, let him cast the first stone at them.[1]

RÜDIGER. (*Crying out in pain.*) Be quiet, I say! Shut up! Have you gone mad!

LEONORE. A horrible pain! Yes! A horrible fate! God knows! But why should I bear this agony all by myself!

RÜDIGER. (*Extreme horror.*) Leonore? The union of our flesh … could you …

LEONORE. I am prepared to go to any lengths! I'll kill myself right now, if that will in any way help you!

RÜDIGER. Kill yourself! Yes? Yes! But … No! The very idea that you are thinking of it …

LEONORE. Do you really mean killing yourself is easier?

RÜDIGER. Easier or not, it does not help!

LEONORE. I'll do whatever you tell me I should do.

RÜDIGER. If I have to tell you what you owe me, then the time is long past when I have any reason to say it.

LEONORE. (*Staring at him.*) I have no answer for that! It's appalling how little we human beings know about our lives, about how we are constantly in a state of joy or terror!

RÜDIGER. With a woman who walks her own path I have nothing to authorize, no commands to give, and nothing to forbid. Even the most virtuously chaste woman does not feel undervalued if she is purchased with two million. God be praised! Then I will be free!

LEONORE. (*Calmly.*) The moment they arrest you, I will shoot myself.

RÜDIGER. I will, too, if it gets that far. I am absolutely sure of that.

1 *And whoever … at them* See John 8.7: "He that is without sin among you, let him first cast a stone at her [a woman accused of adultery]."

SCENE 4

(*Effie enters in a hurry. She is very cheerful.*)

EFFIE. But Mother, Mother, what are you getting so worked up about? I can hear your conversation all the way up in my room. Is that indefatigable foreigner still not satisfied? But you guessed more or less from the beginning that you could someday fall into his devil's claws.

RÜDIGER. The moment a man believes he is bound by something more powerful than his own free will the entire blasphemous horror of marriage is exposed.

LEONORE. (*To Effie.*) Then we can expect no help from your husband?

EFFIE. You mean money? No, dear Mother. My husband has nothing left but debts. Most of the two hundred thousand francs[1] I spent gambling last Wednesday in Monte Carlo didn't come from him. When I left he was busy with a plan to found an Australian railway company. At any rate, he thought there were still no railways in Australia.[2]

LEONORE. What are you intending to live on then?

EFFIE. That will sort itself out. In the first six months we would have drowned ourselves from boredom if I hadn't always made an effort to provide interesting entertainment with my adventures.

RÜDIGER. What is it really that prevents us from living in peace and despising all the mean things we do?

LEONORE. Human dignity prevents us from doing that! Simple dignity, which the poorest child gets as an inheritance from the way his parents remain true to each other! The dignity on which the poorest human being builds his happiness in life!

RÜDIGER. Five minutes ago you were just as decisively asserting the opposite point of view.

LEONORE. And you? Five minutes ago, weren't you just as insistently defending the opposite point of view, as well?

---

1 *francs* Currency of Monaco.

2 *he thought ... in Australia* There had in fact been railways in Australia since the 1850s.

RÜDIGER. I have overcome my lack of conviction and regained my confidence.

LEONORE. Then why were we not in agreement five minutes ago? Why aren't we agreeing now? Should I say it? I understand my child, and I understand you …

RÜDIGER. Leonore, you are so upset, you no longer know what you are saying!

EFFIE. If I were married to a man who was really jealous, I would be willing to help my husband out of such a situation, without damaging my loyalty to him in the slightest.

LEONORE. What do you mean?

EFFIE. I would act as if I were resigning myself to my fate. I would go like a lamb to the slaughter. All of a sudden I would catch fire and become rapturously excited, in love—but all that in such an exaggerated, artificial, and unnatural way that the brute loses all desire, his hair stands on end, and his skin crawls. He has no idea where to turn his head. That way the issue is resolved. Potiphar's wife and Joseph.[1] When he sobers up, the boor's keenest desire is that no living soul ever learns about our meeting.

LEONORE. Child, my child, what is this precipice we have come to?

RÜDIGER. If we consider things calmly, is our situation really so terrible? (*To Leonore.*) In the space of three years I have quadrupled the four hundred thousand marks you received as a dowry from your father. That money is secure. If we can get through today, no one on God's earth will have any more claims against us. Then we will be free and can set off with our minds at ease on whatever paths we both have determined for ourselves. Then I will show people that I had a right to ignore and overstep their boundaries, and in a hundred years the earth will still bear traces of what I have done.

---

1 *Potiphar's wife and Joseph* Reference to the biblical story in Genesis. Potiphar is the captain of the palace guard in Egypt, and Joseph, after being sold into slavery by his brothers, rises to become head of Potiphar's household. Potiphar's wife attempts to seduce Joseph and, when he resists her advances, accuses him of raping her. Joseph is thrown into prison until he is rescued by Pharaoh, who later makes him overlord of Egypt.

LEONORE. Whatever a poor creature like me can do to further your victorious career, I will do. If I don't, have I any right to go on living? I do enough to bring you down and hold you back.

RÜDIGER. Are you perhaps under the impression that in this world great wealth has ever been made in more harmless ways? The first return that every asset immediately brings is the proud advantage that you no longer have to worry where it came from.

EFFIE. I cannot go on living like this any longer. I make a special trip from Monte Carlo to Ouchy to see my parents again, and I find them in a mood that makes me want to put a sack over my head. From morning to night, nothing but difficulties. But I can't sit here all day long by myself up in my room reading Dante.[1] Mother, you are mortally afraid your marriage could be breaking up. But that is just a childish delusion! I know of nothing in the world more indestructible than marriage. And I am not thinking at all about my own. That is so strong and so elastic, it could encompass the world. But I know people who have bickered every day for twenty-five years without ever being unfaithful to each other a single time! And I know people who for twenty-five years have been unfaithful to each other every day without ever quarreling about it even once! No one has any idea of all the things a proper marriage can put up with. It's certainly not at all essential that both people like each other. If only one of the two is fond of the other, that's enough for half a lifetime.

LEONORE. Perhaps I'm not a match for the pressure of events, but I have a sense that I'm being crushed by the situation we face. I feel as if someone has put a foot on my head in order to grind my mouth into the dirt.

EFFIE. That's called hypochondria,[2] dear Mother.

LEONORE. Rüdiger! Do you remember when, in the first three months of our marriage, I came back from Hamburg? You were waiting for me at the railway station in Hannover. As

---

1 *Dante* Italian poet Dante Alighieri (1265–1321), author of *The Divine Comedy.*

2 *hypochondria* Mental disorder characterized by an irrational fear of illness or injury.

soon as we were alone, you told me you had come to the train an hour early. You had walked up and down the platform asking yourself which of two options would be preferable—whether I had let myself be touched by a man's foot under the table in Hamburg or whether on the return journey I had been killed in a railway accident. Back then you stated very firmly that my death would have been preferable.

RÜDIGER. If you asked me that today, my answer would be exactly the same.

LEONORE. For a moment I was confused. But then I thanked my creator that both of us were sufficiently noble to confront the realities of life so fearlessly.

RÜDIGER. Well? And?

LEONORE. And now … ? Now … ?

RÜDIGER. There are thoughts buried deep in one's core that should never be openly talked about, even with married couples. If they start to question whether they belong together, they immediately face each other as deadly enemies.

EFFIE. For me the only people in the world worth paying attention to are the few exceptional ones who make the impossible possible.

LEONORE. The impossible, Effie? It's impossible to give yourself to the murderer of a person you love. I gave myself to him. It's impossible to keep on possessing a man by killing yourself. I am prepared to do that. But to destroy yourself for a man who perhaps does not belong to you anymore … well, that makes me feel like I'm being set upon by packs of dogs!

(*A Waiter enters in a hurry.*)

WAITER. Please excuse me. There is an individual downstairs who claims that Monsieur is going to be threatened by the police.[1]

LEONORE. Now let the entire universe collapse around me!

(*Leonore rushes out. The Waiter looks around wondering what's going on. When he gets no answer, he leaves the room, closing the door behind him.*)

---

1 *Please excuse … the police* In Wedekind's German text, the Waiter's speech is in French.

Scene 5

EFFIE. (*After a pause.*) Are you really from an old noble family?

RÜDIGER. (*Sitting at a table with his head in his hands, groaning.*) I'm completely shattered—only a dreadful caricature of what I used to be.

EFFIE. In a hundred years, no one will understand anymore how we can make such a scandal out of such harmless fun and games.

RÜDIGER. (*Stands up and pulls himself together.*) My mother was born a Goldstaub. She came from Budapest.

EFFIE. I know an ancient prayer. It comes from the time when people were still punished with a lifetime of slavery if two of them got caught embracing in secret. The prayer ends with the words:

> You should not love from weakness
> but from strength,
> from a self-assurance!
> You should not love in darkness
> but in the light.
> Woe for the love
> that vanishes from sight
> when the crowd looks on!
> For as your love is,
> so your children!
> Whoever loves in darkness
> also lives in darkness![1]

RÜDIGER. Where did you read that?

EFFIE. The prayer begins with the words:

> I, the I who is myself . . .
> I always like that line the most!

RÜDIGER. How does it continue?

EFFIE. I, the hidden one

> Who called you into life
> For my own pleasure!

1 *You should ... in darkness* These lines were in fact written by Wedekind himself.

... but there are already omens and miracles happening. I know an American who champions the people. He has made it his life's work to free relationships between men and women from all medieval instruments of torture.

RÜDIGER. I know who you mean. I am familiar with the enchanting eloquence of his writing.

EFFIE. A dry old stick as a lover! But my powers of endurance—which I have not yet found in any of my sisters! I think of myself as an inexplicable natural wonder. One moonlit night in the Coliseum in Rome the age I should really have lived in became clear to me—either the time of Pericles in Athens or, even better, in Corinth, or else in Rome under Commodus or Caracalla.[1]

RÜDIGER. You are so superhumanly proud of your profession. I don't know any diplomat who would take more pride in his lack of responsibility.

EFFIE. Surrendering ourselves is our particular view of the world. I thought about this for two years, until the scales fell from my eyes one morning. It was on a lonely mountain top in Upper Austria. I was all alone waiting for the sun to rise. As the first sparks of light punctured the steel-blue screen I asked myself, What is the greatest triumph sought by a woman who has no children? Sensual experience!

RÜDIGER. You could have miscalculated. Remember Goethe's lines:[2]

> Man remains desirable until from life he parts,
> but woman shrivels up before her reasoning starts.

EFFIE. (*Sings.*)

> A child I know is a delight,
> a very rare and lovely sight.
> Her eyes are black and black her hair,
> her build and bearing truly fair.

---

1 *the time ... or Caracalla* Historical ages which are famous for (among other things) the beauty, power, and influence of certain prostitutes.

2 *Goethe's lines* Johann Wolfgang (von) Goethe (1749–1832), the leading German poet of his time. These lines were in fact written by Wedekind, not Goethe.

She's not too thin and not too small
and not too fat and not too tall.
Her songs and dances make her glad,
And even now she drives men mad.

And then there's that other poem by Goethe:

(*Effie begins singing and dancing.*)

Are your muscles tense and braced,
your shoes and stockings all in place,
then in the center of the throng
begin the dance.
Front and back a royal queen!
Dance like no woman ever danced.
With every movement that you can
Left leg,
Nimble leg,
The right must even nimbler be!

Perhaps you know which classical composer wrote this song:

The young girl is so fair
with legs beyond compare,
a model for the rest,
in all the world the best.

And best of all to tell,
she leapt around so well,
while her legs danced their art
she sprang into my heart.

RÜDIGER. Your singing is delightful. I'm waiting for your reply.

EFFIE. Just be patient. Our adventures demand intelligence and skill, in equal amounts. Two weeks ago in one and the same evening I dined in Monte Carlo with three different gentlemen at the same time in the same hotel, without any of them knowing anything about the presence of the other two. That was emotional gymnastics! I had to keep track of every second.

I invented excuses for my departures and for keeping each one waiting. So much so, my head was whirling like a mechanized spinning factory. Each one of the gentlemen picked me up where we were staying, and each of them ordered a different five-course dinner. I did not let a single one get taken away without tasting it. Each one brought me back in a car to our residence. It was a confused jumble of delicious mouthfuls, popping corks, car rides, and squandering money on tips … The waiters oversaw the entire business as delighted spectators. I have never yet been served more respectfully and with more ceremonious expressions in any hotel. What an effort that cost me, when the next day I had to sort out once again all the different events, arguments, and surprises in their appropriate compartments! I still felt a champagne fog in my head—otherwise I'd have drawn up a statistical chart.

RÜDIGER. (*He has recovered his composure.*) After this masterstroke in Monte Carlo was your life still safe?

EFFIE. Why would that concern me? But picture to yourself what happened afterwards! The next day, as evening approaches, the three gentlemen go, as usual, to the Casino. Each of them explains to a large circle of friends he has carefully gathered around him that yesterday at eleven o'clock he had an intimate dinner in the Hotel Méditérrané with the celebrated Countess d'Armont, or Little Monkey, as they call me. The gentlemen furthest away from those telling the story hear all three reports at once. They keep quiet for quite a while, enjoying themselves on their own. Suddenly the entire Casino room bursts into resounding laughter. My three lovers have naturally hated each other for a long time, just like fathers of the church. At first, they look as if they've been struck by lightning. All at once from three different sides the shouting starts: You liar! You liar! You liar! Each one challenges the other two to a duel with pistols. Finally, a fearful brawl breaks out. I had been expecting that. As the bloody heads were cooling off with ice water, I let myself be escorted through the room by Herzog von Eurasburg. No one dared make the slightest remark about me. I said to myself, how pathetically small the whole world looks when it lies at my feet.

RÜDIGER. (*At Effie's side.*) There is a moist look shimmering in your dark eyes. It's fascinating. I've never seen it any other woman.

EFFIE. I will give you a present of one night ...

RÜDIGER. I am not in the market.

EFFIE. One single night ...

RÜDIGER. But I don't want to fight it out with waiters!

EFFIE. But not tonight ...

RÜDIGER. Too bad!

EFFIE. I don't yet know which one ...

RÜDIGER. My time is my own to do as I please.

EFFIE. But when this night comes, I will kiss you so you will never forget me anymore during your lifetime.

(*A shot cracks out from the floor below.*)

RÜDIGER. (*Trembling with shock.*) What was that?

EFFIE. A revolver! What else could it be?

RÜDIGER. Then something bad has happened!

EFFIE. Why would you say that?

RÜDIGER. You can still ask that question?

(*Rüdiger exits.*)

EFFIE. (*Alone.*) Something bad does not happen as easily as that! And what if it does! There are always beneficial consequences, too. How worried people are about disaster! For me each day can bring catastrophe. When would I be safe from simple murder? One more thrill! Fate, how I thank you for preparing me so extravagantly for this career! No getting tired! No breaking down! No inhibitions! No obsessions! No hangovers!

Scene 6

(*Rüdiger leads Leonore into the room. She is having trouble holding herself upright.*)

Effie. (*With a shrill cry.*) Mother! (*She runs to Leonore.*) Merciful Heaven, you look dreadful!

Leonore. Effie? … Are you still alive?

Rüdiger. (*Trembling with worry, setting Leonore into an armchair.*) Pull yourself together, for God's sake! Lie down and rest.

Leonore. The staircase up to here! The staircase! It never ended! One wall after another!

Effie. What was it? What happened?

Rüdiger. He shot himself!

Effie. (*Kneeling next to her mother.*) Shot? He shot himself? With you there?

Leonore. You planted the idea in me, Effie!

Rüdiger. Forget that! You shouldn't be listening to people talking for a week!

Effie. I was showing off, Mother, exaggerating with childish fantasies!

Leonore. I stagger down there … each step, each landing an impassable wall. (*Crying out.*) And now he is lying there!

Rüdiger. Come to your senses. If you think back on it, you'll kill yourself.

Effie. Should I call the doctor, Mother? Should I bring you something stronger?

Rüdiger. (*Stroking Leonore anxiously.*) What's done is done! Think! You must get through this for our sakes! You look as if you didn't have a drop of blood left in your body!

Leonore. Your freedom has been bought with blood! Be proud, Rüdiger! Set yourself beside those whose heads wear royal crowns! Your freedom has been bought with two human lives!

Rüdiger. God in Heaven, with two!

Leonore. Perhaps in your reckoning mine counts for nothing? How quickly that made you flinch! Do you count my life as nothing? What am I now? No, you have not suffered!

EFFIE. What man ever came into a woman's room in such despair! And all because we women do not know the power we possess!

LEONORE. Child! Child! God protect us from that power! He was looking out the window whistling some tune. And the hellish fear that the brute would throw himself on top of me. I go at him. You are lost! I am lost! He is planted by the mirror, deliberately tying himself up in his cravat. Now one last effort. I force myself to laugh ... laugh ... laugh (*She breaks out in wild laughter.*) I want you! I order ... demand! I swear to enjoy you! Now you can ... to your heart's content ... make love to me!

RÜDIGER. (*Striking his temples with his fists.*) Will this agonizing torture never end?

LEONORE. Well, that wiped the insolence from his face right away! And his crudeness disappeared! His intoxication with victory dissolved! And his laughter stuck in his throat before it could break out! And then ...

RÜDIGER. Hurry up, Leonore! Is this story of how I was saved going to destroy my reason?

LEONORE. He is choking on his own curses. White as plaster, he bares his teeth. And me? I should be beaten into pieces, trampled on, crushed! (*With her hands covering her face she sinks into another chair.*)

EFFIE. (*In a muffled but firm tone, to Rüdiger.*) You will be committing an inhuman crime if you still keep tormenting this woman now!

RÜDIGER. Would it perhaps be more loving if I listened with indifference?

LEONORE. (*With tears streaming down her face.*) What did I do then that was so terrible? I kissed him, so he might kick me around. But then ... (*Suddenly composed, without tears, staring first at Rüdiger and then at Effie.*) ... then he pulls ... pulls both hands back over his own head—I can still feel his fists burning on my cheeks—then he jerks a bit ... he had shot himself from above back through his head. (*Pointing to the top of her head.*) He had shot himself here! (*Staggering back.*) He falls against my knees so I fall back onto the fireplace ... just lies there without moving. (*Pause.*)

SCENE 7

(*Van Zeeter, the manager of the hotel, enters the room quickly.*)

VAN ZEETER. This is obviously extremely distressing for me, but I must ask you ladies and gentlemen as firmly as possible to avoid making any unnecessary noise. I have placed our private automobile at your immediate disposal. I cannot do more than that. The car is waiting in the second courtyard by the backstairs. (*He opens the door and calls out.*) Quickly Monsieur Duvoisin. Hurry up. Let's finish this. We won't make too much noise! (*He allows Monsieur Duvoisin and two policemen to come into the room, and points to Leonore.*) There is the lady in question![1]

DUVOISON. (*To Leonore.*) Madame, I am the prefect of police for the town of Ouchy. Are you Madame Wetterstein? Is that not true, Madame? Madame, you are under arrest. Follow me!

EFFIE. What's going on?

VAN ZEETER. (*To Effie.*) The death penalty is no longer enforced in this canton. So the lady does not need to worry too much. But leave here as quickly as you can. Today we are having a large concert here in the evening featuring Catalani[2] from Paris.

EFFIE. You do realize that this is a case of suicide.

VAN ZEETER. Forgive me, I don't know anything at all. (*To Duvoisin.*) All right, Monsieur Duvoisin, let's close this case!

DUVOISON. Madame, you are obliged to follow me to the prefecture of police. Hurry up, Madame![3]

RÜDIGER. (*To Leonore.*) You will be released immediately—there's no doubt about that at all.

LEONORE. I am going to prison, Effie? Effie,

---

1 *There is ... in question* In Wedekind's text the hotel manager speaks in French to the hotel employees and to the police.

2 *Catalani* Perhaps Alfredo Catalani (1854–93), Italian operatic composer. If that is the person referred to here, then this name provides a clue as to the approximate date of the action.

3 *Madame ... Madame* In Wedekind's text Duvoison speaks French to Leonore here.

is this your work? Help me, Almighty One,
help me get over this appalling force,
the power of women! No, Rüdiger,
I am still too good, however poor I am,
to force myself on you. Love one another!
Today the poorest mortal human being
no longer pities me! Why should the child
feel any trace of pity for its mother
or the husband any pity for his wife!
Love each other! Love each other! Perhaps,
in ages yet to come, men will view my crime
with milder eyes. I cannot force myself
on you when I am stained with blood.
Don't lay a hand on me. I'm off to prison!

(*Leonore leaves the room, moving quickly.*)

ACT 3

(*A low but spacious snow-white paneled room with a white wooden ceiling. The main doorway is downstage right [from the audience's viewpoint].*[1] *In the middle of the back wall there is a doorway covered with white curtains decorated with a pattern of roses in full bloom, and downstage left there is a small door with a pointed arch, hardly noticeable in the white wainscot panelling. On both side-walls between the side doors and the back wall is a row of low, wide windows close to each other. Through the windows of the right side-wall, one can see the inside of a large, sunlit medieval castle courtyard and through the windows on the left side wall a few slender tree tops, the top of a small watchtower, and above that the deep blue sky. The windows on the courtyard side are closed, while those on the facing*

1 *A low … audience's viewpoint* In these stage directions, and in the rest of this act, Wedekind abandons his habit of describing the scene and the actor's movement from the point of view of the actors looking out at the audience, switching instead to the view of the stage from the audience's point of view.

wall are wide open. The furniture in the room consists of three small tables with flimsy chairs around them, all blindingly white. There is no rocking chair, sofa, or settee. The tables are set for tea. There is a samovar[1] *on the middle table. When the curtains on the middle door are open, one can see into a room lit with a dull red glow, without being able to recognize any particular details.*)

Scene I

(*Heiri Wipf, in shirtsleeves,*[2] *wearing a green apron and a gigantic hat made out of rushes with a red band around it, is taking fresh fruit out of a crude wicker basket and filling fruit bowls set on the tables.*)

HEIRI WIPF. (*Singing.*)

O, the plums were so blue!
O, the plums were so blue!

PROFESSOR SCHARLACH. (*Opening the door downstage right and calling into the room.*) Hey, you good-for-nothing, no more songs! The tunes are catchy, but they're too damn loud!

Heiri Wipf . (*Laughing.*) That would be something totally new for me! (*He goes towards Scharlach with his fist raised.*) You perjured heretic! Why should I not keep singing here?

SCHARLACH. Be quiet! The mistress of the castle is not well.

HEIRI WIPF. What? The mistress of the castle? Our dear young mistress? Does she have a pain somewhere?

SCHARLACH. Of course, she's in pain! If not, she wouldn't cry.

HEIRI WIPF. She's crying? O my God! The mistress of the castle weeps! Damn it, why didn't you tell me right away? O you worn out fool! If the young mistress of the castle weeps, it must be something bad!

SCHARLACH. It is! And now get out of here!

---

1 *samovar* Metal tea urn, often ornately decorated, originating in Russia.

2 *in shirtsleeves* I.e., not wearing a coat; in informal attire.

HEIRI WIPF. That's far from a good excuse for you to talk so rudely to me! You burned up, worn-out heretic! Be sure you tell the mistress of the castle Heiri Wipf sends the young lady his best wishes for a quick recovery!

(*Heiri Wipf leaves downstage right. Professor Scharlach follows him out.*)

SCENE 2

(*Professor Scharlach leads Effie into the room. She is wearing an evening dress and a tiara. Her face is streaming tears, and she is sobbing almost uncontrollably. He takes her to one of the open windows. Still weeping, she sinks down on a chair in front of it.*)

SCHARLACH. (*Sighing.*) O dear, O dear, O dear, O dear, O dear![1]
Such a disastrous dolt! Who would have thought
it would turn out like this. Swept away
by my discoveries in medicine
and without thinking what I'm doing,
I forcefully inject my murderous idea
into my guinea pig, right in her heart!
EFFIE. (*Howling.*) I built myself a way to see the world.
O God, O God, how much of that remains,
my silly childish vision of the world!

(*She cries as if her heart were breaking.*)

SCHARLACH. It is not good for you, my child, to let
your agitation run with no restraint.
EFFIE. (*Howling.*) My pride, my arrogance, my sense of fun,
the freedom of my life as an adventurer,
for that I thanked the way I see the world.
For every glance I used to snare a man,
for every night I spent in sensual riot,
I've kept a faithful personal account,
as if I had become a manager
entrusted with a piece of property.

1 From here until the end of the play, the German text is set primarily as unrhymed verse rather than as prose.

And now I hear it's all just a disease,
my desire is disease, my eyes disease,
and my vitality only a disease!

SCHARLACH. (*Sighing.*) My room up here, the one I'm living in,
gets the most sun and is the coziest
in all the castle. You're the one, Effie,
I have to thank for that. Every morning
the young girl brings me breakfast to my bed,
and I ask myself if I'm still dreaming
a dream of childhood. Below my window
there is a noise from where the rabbits live,
while across the way, caressed by sunlight
and by ivy stands, the red-brown quadrant
of the castle keep. Effie, you should not
be ungrateful for such a magic realm.
You are enthroned here like a sovereign mistress
in your baronial seat, a way of life
unknown to anyone for centuries.

EFFIE. (*Drying her tears.*) And this is something you have now prepared
for me to swallow, today of all days,
when, more so now than ever, I still need
my sense of humor, idiocy, and folly,
my vision of the world. And yet today
it's all collapsing, crushing me to death!

SCHARLACH. Who knows, my child, if there is not a sign
of Heaven in this. Out of respect for you
for one week now I have been holding back
from openly discussing it with you.
The rest of us, who are all satellites
encircling you, providing you protection,
all of us for once are in agreement …

EFFIE. (*Calmly and firmly.*) Enough, enough. It is impossible
for me to talk about it. Anyway,
it's not a thing the public can decide.
So now please tell me—make it short and sweet—
what I heard and only partly understood
because I was in shock. My strong desires,

if I understand correctly, arise
from illnesses in my digestive tract?

SCHARLACH. (*Shrugging his shoulders.*) From childhood on, it seems, you wore corsets
and laced them up too tight.

EFFIE. So this gleam in my eyes,
which makes a man a promise of some kind,
I owe that to a problem with my liver?

SCHARLACH. You know, Effie, how ruthless I must be
to whip my work in medical research
through every net, if I'm ever going to land
the smallest catch that offers evidence.
Twelve years now I've been working on my book
called "Criminality: Its Preconditions."
Not that I became your personal physician
merely because I wished to spy on you.
The fee that Salzmann is now paying me
would have attracted someone else first rate.
But is it then all that astonishing
if, in the middle of the noisy chatter
of the conversation at our midday meal,
for one single moment I could forget
the purpose of the universe is you,
not science.

EFFIE. And my face changes color
so easily and fast, my skin is dull.
Do all these symptoms come from gall stones,
or is the cause some sickness in the lungs?

SCHARLACH. (*With the most affectionate concern.*) In future, Effie, no man you look at
will be able to resist—he will be
completely at your mercy. That's the truth.
Just as it's true there is no living man
who knows how to flatter that pride of yours
more shamelessly than me. You must stay calm!
I hear the noble champions of your empire
already climbing up the stairs. Be happy!
No one must know that you're not feeling well.

EFFIE. (*Getting up.*) Life's glorious flame has been extinguished,
and nothing now remains but joyless ash.
To expiate one's sins by selling sex,
the rationalization of a whore,
how shockingly insipid and idiotic
that now sounds. But I will not turn back.
Decline and dissolution are approaching,
but they will find me standing strong and proud,
the way I looked when I was fortunate.

SCENE 3

(*Rüdiger von Wetterstein opens the door downstage right and sticks his head into the room.*)

RÜDIGER. May we come in, my child?
EFFIE. Yes, yes, please do.
RÜDIGER. (*In the open doorway, calling back outside.*) Come in, dear heart. We're not disturbing her.
LEONORE VON WETTERSTEIN. (*Entering.*) My dear child! Good heavens, have you been crying?
EFFIE. (*Excessively cheerful.*) I've been laughing till my eyes filled up with tears.
No, dear mother, if you'd heard the story
Hannibal just told and understood it,
you'd be on your back, howling with laughter.
LEONORE. (*Embracing Effie.*) O Effie, to find you in this cheerful mood
is such a comfort to me. Do you know
the princely gift you offered us today?
(*To Rüdiger.*) May I mention it?
RÜDIGER. It's not up to me
to tell my fate's companion what to say.
I don't give her orders or forbid things,
not after I have scattered all she owns
to the four winds and seen how that hard work
has made my head turn bald.
LEONORE. And like a young girl

you still fish for compliments! My hair is white,
but not because I worked so frantically.
The first early post today delivered
a contract fully signed, assuring us
an annual income, guaranteed for life.
Rüdiger and I, from this day forward,
each year receive ... (*To Rüdiger.*) May I state the sum?

RÜDIGER. ... eight thousand marks! Professor Scharlach
has already gained our daughter's confidence.

LEONORE. (*To Effie.*) My child, my child, what must that have cost you!

EFFIE. A mere conjuring trick!

LEONORE. But Karl Salzmann
seems to be helped by supernatural spirits.

RÜDIGER. Ah yes, a good man, Salzmann! In a dream
I'd never have imagined I would be
a guest again in my ancestral home.

LEONORE. Here in Castle Wetterstein! It sounds grand—
Rüdiger von Wetterstein in Wetterstein![1]

RÜDIGER. In Salzmann Guesthouse, Castle Wetterstein,
by contrast, has a much more modern ring.

SCHARLACH. And if sometimes perhaps Director Salzmann
seems radical in treatments he applies,
one must acknowledge with the highest praise
the gift he has for organizing things!

RÜDIGER. A perfect businessman! I can't believe
what he thinks up, the range of his ideas!

LEONORE. (*To Effie.*) And what a sensitive and lovely home
he's made for us, me and your father,
inside the tower—two secret hidden steps lead up
into our bower, like some higher world.
Far to the north, the dark high regions
of the Schwarzwald,[2] and outside our windows

---

1 *in Wetterstein* The Wetterstein is also a group of mountains in the eastern Alps.

2 *Schwarzwald* German: Black Forest; a large, well-forested mountain range in southwestern Germany, alongside the Rhine.

right above the entranceway, the courtyard,
originally built in sixteen thirty-two.
It's unbelievable! But here he comes!

SCENE 4

(*Karl Salzmann, Waldemar Uhlhorst, Matthias Taubert, and Schigabet enter. Schigabet has a mad hairstyle (à la Wahnsinn*[1]*), and is wearing a stiff shirt collar, bow tie, lace shirt cuffs, a blue frock coat, gold vest, purple knee breeches, silver-gray silk stockings, and leather shoes with buckles and red heels. He is carrying a troubadour's lute under his arm.*)

SALZMANN. Come on then, let's have a cup of coffee!
Here everyone feels less inhibited
than when they are at home.

(*He turns to Effie as the others come in.*)

In Yokohama
the World's Fair will be opening in May.[2]
But still, I wonder if we might prefer
to visit the South Pole. I have a hunch,
Effie, that absolutely everyone
who's anyone in the world will gather
this coming summer at the southern pole.

EFFIE. I think we should see the World's Fair first
and then, after that, go to the South Pole.

SALZMANN. Thank you, my little treasure.

EFFIE. This Mister Tschamper—
where in the castle is he going to stay?

SALZMANN. In the old armory, south-west from here.
The morning sun comes in there from the yard
and, at sunset, sinks behind the furthest peak.

---

1 *à la Wahnsinn* French and German: in the style of madness.

2 *the World's Fair … May* A fictional reference; no World's Fair was held in Yokohama (though one was held in nearby Tokyo in 1877).

EFFIE. And if he walks across the yard at noon
up to the parapet, the ageless ice
of Jungfrau's[1] glacial face will gleam at him.
SALZMANN. Fanfares of trumpets will announce to us
Mister Tschamper's entry through the gate
of the lower courtyard. In the gallery
we have placed musicians with hunting horns.
Then in the castle courtyard Schigabet
will make a formal welcoming address.
SCHIGABET. Yes, of course, provided Mister Tschamper
has sorted out my guest performances
in Argentina. Comedians like me,
so people say, in times like these can do
brilliant business in South America.
EFFIE. (*Clapping her hands.*) Now Schigabet will sing a brand new song!
SCHIGABET. You want a song? While all those here must wait
to see this thousand-year-old pile of stone
fly up into the air, and us as well?
EFFIE. The time till Mister Tschamper reaches us
will fly past much more quickly.
RÜDIGER. Time up here
sprints past at such a terrifying speed,
even in the absence of explosions,
day and night I have irrational fears
the earth could leap out from its orbit.
LEONORE. For God's sake, Rüdiger, don't joke so lightly
about this ancient globe of ours.
RÜDIGER. But then,
my dearest heart, we'd get the benefit
of leaving this lovely world together.
LEONORE. The one remaining happiness I pray for!
TAUBERT. A pile of stones? Explosions? Is the castle
in danger of being blown to smithereens?
UHLHORST. In the anarchists' laboratory

1 *Jungfrau* Well-known mountain in the Swiss Alps; the name means "maiden" or "virgin."

on the ground floor, which I myself installed,
this morning early I rigged up a bomb
as an experiment to see if it would work.
If it suddenly explodes, all on its own,
and blows us up, the bomb is useless.
But if its violence can be locked in
and released at our command, then people
no longer need to be afraid of armies,
they'll have floods and earthquakes made to order,
and no thief thundering with his artillery
will get away without being punished.

SCHIGABET. (*Sings and plays his lute.*)
In secret catacombs
we fabricate our bombs
as the old curse foretold.
Heavenly elements and bombs!

EFFIE. I've not yet ever possessed a lover
whose acrobatic vocal chords could sing
a coloratura[1] as well as Schigabet.

UHLHORST. (*In an armchair, with one leg over the other.*) We three—you, Effie, Taubert, and I—
all contradict our valued social order.
You, Effie, dancing girl and prostitute;
Matthias Taubert, a metaphysician
propped up by man's mental laziness;
and I, who for high stakes would happily
hazard my life, if it were somehow possible
simply to be rid of it without dishonor.

EFFIE. (*Clapping her hands.*) Now Schigabet will sing a brand new song!

LEONORE. (*Kissing Effie on the forehead.*) Don't let us disturb you, my dear child.
Your father and I are going to seek
some peace and quiet for an hour or so.

RÜDIGER. In the mulberry tree outside our window

1 *coloratura* Elaborate vocal melody.

blackbirds chirp a lullaby.
UHLHORST. As a child,
you have already listened to those songs.
Isn't Castle Wetterstein your home?
RÜDIGER. No, not at all. I was born in Berlin,
Steglitzerstrasse—number forty-six.
I went from there to school for young cadets.
Not since the thirteenth century has my family
owned this castle. And now, gentlemen,
you must excuse me. In this whole place
I am the only worn out married man.
LEONORE. But look at how our marriage has withstood
so many trials and storms and how happy
and indestructible it still remains!
RÜDIGER. Only because at last you understand,
Leonore, what in life has lasting value.
LEONORE. Like sipping coffee in the afternoon,
eyes half-closed, no need to think at all.
SALZMANN. (*To Rüdiger.*) Herr Baron, would you allow me to serve
you and the baroness an evening meal
in your hidden honeysuckle bower?
LEONORE. (*Squeezing Salzmann's hand.*) What a splendid man you are, Salzmann!
SALZMANN. I wish the two of you a pleasant rest.

(*Rüdiger and Leonore leave downstage right.*)

EFFIE. (*Clapping her hands.*) Now Schigabet will sing a brand new song!
SCHIGABET. (*Singing and playing his lute.*)
On the steamship
It smells of camphor.[1]
Who brings that smell on board?
No one except some wealthy lord!

1 *camphor* Natural substance derived from a tree, which has long been used as a medicine for a wide variety of medical conditions, especially sexual ailments. It has a very distinctive smell.

SALZMANN. You should try that song in Argentina!
It will bring magnificent success.
Once Mister Tschamper listens to you sing,
he'll have to take you. You may have deep roots
in Europe, but he'll tear you away.
TAUBERT. (*Sitting in an armchair.*) Up here I had an unexpected pleasure.
It was quite bizarre. The torture chamber
in which I'm writing my "City of the Sun"[1]
is so cut off from the castle courtyard
on such an isolated craggy rock,
only the view towards the south provides
me any company. But in that place
a blissful feeling overpowers me
when I think of the enormous pain
people once suffered in this narrow space ...
Often the joy I feel is so intense
I find it hard to keep my self-control.
EFFIE. I once knew a man who in the evening
scattered bits of glass across his bed.
He was afraid that one night without warning
he might die of boredom while asleep.
UHLHORST. In the year
eleven fifty Friedrich Barbarossa
rode up here seeking to catch his rival,
Count Ulerich, and break him on the wheel.[2]
In those years, historically speaking,
anarchism had come into full bloom.
I say this remembering that at the time
the moral order of the world resembled
almost perfectly what we have today

---

1 *City of the Sun* Philosophical utopian work by Tommaso Campanella published in Latin in 1623 in Frankfurt.

2 *Friedrich Barbarossa ... the wheel* Frederick I (1122–90) was King of Germany, King of Italy, and Holy Roman Emperor, and was known as a great and powerful leader; it is unclear to whom "his rival, / Count Ulerich," refers; *wheel* Instrument of torture.

with our "Propaganda of the Deed,"[1]
so much so that we might praise ourselves
and boast that we are truly heroes.

EFFIE. But in this ancient princely residence
I am the only person who can boast
of any contact with true nobility.
Matthias, after your excommunication
by the Holy See,[2] you finally became
a famous man, but did you stay in touch,
even by letter? As for you, Waldemar,
floods and earthquakes, so people say, obey
what you command. But even that power
brings you no closer to the rulers of the earth.
At best, you'll earn yourself a hero's death
battling before a judge or the police.
When I think of the riotous excitement,
screams of joy from a thousand, thousand hearts,
every time the one I love goes riding
from his residence and smiles, on his way
to some public festival, I count myself
much happier than all those other women
whimpering in their family prison cells.[3]

---

1 *Propaganda of the Deed* Overtly political acts designed to inspire others. The phrase gained currency in the late nineteenth and early twentieth centuries, particularly among anarchist groups, to express the notion that significant political ideas arise from actions (including especially acts of violence) rather than the other way around.

2 *Holy See* Holy Seat; i.e., the Roman Catholic Church.

3 *When I … prison cells* The "lover" Effie refers to here and throughout the scene seems clearly modeled on Crown Prince Frederick William Victor of Prussia (1859–1941), heir to the throne of Prussia (and after 1871 to the new German Empire). He was married in 1881 and had several children. He succeeded his father (who reigned for only ninety-nine days) in 1888. If we are to take Effie's details about her lover as indicating someone presently alive, then the action in this scene apparently takes place in the mid 1880s (i.e., before William became the new Kaiser, but after his marriage and the birth of his first children).

TAUBERT. Come on then! Uhlhorst, Scharlach, Schigabet,
and Salzmann! Let's slit our bellies open!
What low and lazy wretches we have been
to find that we are placed here on God's earth
without a single drop of royal blood!
EFFIE. God in Heaven, such a beautiful man!
And yet no fool. The free and royal way
he uses to express himself. All you here
have pet names for me. Schigabet calls me
"My little monkey," and you, Karl Salzmann,
as we all know, call me "My little treasure,"
while Uhlhorst says "My pony." Matthias Taubert
uses the nickname "Epiphania,"
and Scharlach christens me "My guinea pig."
When my prince observed me at the races
driving my white-eyed black-horse team and glimpsed
the fleshy color of their sexual parts,
he gave a loud shout to his adjutant,
"By the sacramental cross, look at that—
see how those horse cocks match that pair of eyes!"
SCHIGABET. My little monkey, why is it your prince
does not hire me as his comedian?
SCHARLACH. And me as his physician?
TAUBERT. Or me
as his confessor?
SALZMANN. Me as finance minister?
UHLHORST. And me as chancelor?
EFFIE. Because my lover
must love me purely and simply for myself—
entirely for me! Where he's concerned,
I do not wish to owe you anything
for your intellectual talents! Not you
or any earthly power! I thank myself,
the way I was created, for his love.
To prevent a world war breaking out

the prince got married.[1] But to me he brings
his unspent passion. He is a man for whom,
when he is on horseback, women in droves,
even the most beautiful, hurl themselves
beneath his horses' hooves. And for this man
I am the loftiest summit of the world.
After our first conversation he sent me
the golden cup from which we both had drunk,
the most precious thing I own. Until today,
I have never found sufficient time
to decipher the engraving on it.

(*Effie takes the cup out of a small box, which she has fetched from a cupboard and gives it to Uhlhorst.*)

UHLHORST. (*Slowly deciphering the inscription on the cup.*) Come
… what … come … may … .
All … things … will … pass … away.
(*To Effie.*) But what does his royal eminence think
about the way you view the world? Your prince
must find it awkward, when in the middle
of the most delightful sensual passion,
he has to rush around, trying to find
a bunch of brand spanking new ideas.

EFFIE. But just think, Waldemar, a man like him!
A ruler without flaw, from head to toe
perfect in every way, just like Achilles![2]
So I can chatter on however I wish—
the silliest jokes will not topple him

1 *To prevent … got married* Wilhelm II married Augusta Victoria of Schleswig-Holstein in 1881, a match resisted in some quarters but very much favored by the German Chancelor Otto von Bismark, on the grounds that it would relieve tension between Prussia and the Duke of Schleswig-Holstein (the bride's father). The Duke's territory had been annexed by Prussia and Austria in 1864 and later by Prussia alone in 1866. For a number of years, this political situation was complex and potentially a great threat to European peace.

2 *Achilles* Greek hero of the Trojan War, considered by legend to have been the greatest warrior in Greece.

from his high place. When I romanticize,
without a single word of blasphemy,
the holy ritual of the embrace,
as if he were a royal libertine,
he hears me out and never bats an eye.
He is so pleased when I play hide-and-seek,
a female game to keep our men in chains.

TAUBERT. It seems unlikely that you'd tell your prince
about the stages on our ladder of love.[1]

EFFIE. Sometimes, while deep in a dream, he mutters
something about the ladder of love. And once,
when he was visiting Torpedo Harbor[2]
and christening a ship, he could not read
the speech a person had just handed him,
and, without pausing long to think, he said

First in darkness, second lit by lamps
such cruel suffering for slavish tramps.

UHLHORST. Third in the daylight, fourth in open air,
Joys that even in death do not bring despair!

SALZMANN. Fifth completely naked, sixth in mirror frames—
how those tempests quicken senses once again!

TAUBERT. Seventh clothed in pearls, eighth for something grand,
the sins of servitude have long been banned!

EFFIE. Ninth in competition, tenth sacrificial rite,
so that we never lose our sacred light.

---

1 *ladder of love* Traditional Christian concept (German: Liebesstufenleiter) of a series of steps (often ten) leading the soul from earthly concerns up to a love of God. Wedekind's images of that ladder here are characteristically secular. This passage inspired a series of erotic etchings (by E.L., probably Rudolf Lamm) published in 1920, entitled *Liebesstufenleiter von Frank Wedekind.*

2 *Torpedo Harbor* Wilhelmshaven, the most important naval base in Imperial Germany.

SCHIGABET. (*Tuning his lute.*) I have written a side-splitting parody
of our ladder of love. You'll double up
with laughter when you hear my verse!

(*A solemn fanfare of hunting horns, interspersed with the loud sounds of automobile horns becomes audible from outside.*)

SALZMANN. Those are the horns of Mister Chagnaral!
All of us should go out in the courtyard
to welcome Mister Chagnaral Tschamper
from Atakama[1] to Castle Wetterstein!
SCHIGABET. After your speech of welcome, will you please
recommend me to him for Argentina.
SALZMANN. That will be done! For Mister Tschamper's entry
into the upper hall, we should prepare
a greeting no benefactor of the world
has ever seen up here, not since the time
that Barbarossa visited this place!

(*They all leave the room, except for Effie and Taubert.*)

SCENE 5

EFFIE. Why are you not attending the reception
for Mister Tschamper?
TAUBERT. I have no wish to see him.
I leave today. How long will he be here?
EFFIE. He's reserved a room with us for thirty days.
TAUBERT. Epiphania! You need to take great care
with this old goat! He has already killed
three or four prostitutes.
EFFIE. (*Laughing.*) Newspaper stories!
If even one were true, he would not be free
to move around.
TAUBERT. According to reports,
the girls all killed themselves.
EFFIE. Then they were stupid.

---

1 *Atakama* The Atacama Desert, a long stretch of land on the Pacific coast of Chile in South America. It is the driest non-polar desert in the world.

And you yourself concede he did not kill them.
TAUBERT. How much money does he pay to have his fun?
EFFIE. One hundred thousand dollars.
TAUBERT. Good for him!
EFFIE. That is the highest price anyone has paid
for me so far.
TAUBERT. Still, you shouldn't take it.
Epiphania, it's wiser to refuse.
EFFIE. How can I? If, once again, the Prince
cannot repay his debts, then the Kaiser
will declare he is unfit to manage
his affairs, the regional assembly
will then appropriate his principality,
bypassing the authority of regent,
and make it part of all imperial lands.
They will appoint someone as governor.
A dynasty that's reigned a thousand years
will cease to rule!
TAUBERT. Only to be ruled by you!
And then, at last, you'll have him to yourself.
EFFIE. No, just the opposite! If he renounces
his succession to the throne, I'm done for.
Then he'll live only for his wife and children.
TAUBERT. Is he that business-like about such things?
EFFIE. He is not as free as you are. The Princess
wrote to me herself. And in addition,
he only gets two hundred thousand marks.
Karl Salzmann gets one hundred thousand—
his payment for drawing up the contract
with Mister Tschamper so unambiguously,
he cannot under any circumstances
demand to have my fee returned to him.
In our line of business, that is always
the most challenging problem of them all.
TAUBERT. You get to keep one hundred thousand marks?
EFFIE. Provided I fulfill what we've agreed—
the stipulated duties. Otherwise
I get nothing. I needed more than that

to secure my parents an annuity.
Karl Salzmann undertook the personal task
of buying that annuity and showed
so much expert knowledge that my father
goes into raptures when he talks of it.
TAUBERT. His history tells us that two young girls
ended their lives while he was watching.
EFFIE. The Argentinian has a single wish—
to die while resting in a woman's arms.
And that, in the end, is not astonishing.
A hundred men would not have found the strength
to kill themselves, if, before that moment,
in their relationships with women
they had never felt the disgust with life
which always plays a role in suicides.
TAUBERT. Well, it still appears to me suspicious
that up to now he's not had much success.
EFFIE. In our profession, there are abject creatures,
thousands of them, who cannot bring themselves
to witness a man's death. They have no idea
of the power we have to control men's fate.
TAUBERT. How many deaths have you seen up to now?
EFFIE. My husband shot himself here on my heart.
TAUBERT. Epiphania Aphrodisiaca![1]
Whenever you make a night-time visit
to a graveyard, the coffin lids rise up.
But you must take great care.
EFFIE. (*Laughing.*) What is it
I need to be afraid of? Last summer
I spent my time cooped up in Mondsee[2]
with an Afghani prince, who was quite mad,
a summer stay like all the others.

1 *Aphrodisiaca* Name for an unknown precious stone. The word is also sometimes used in the botanical name for plants with allegedly aphrodisiac qualities (e.g., Turnera diffusa var aphrodisiaca).

2 *Mondsee* Town and region by the shores of a lake in a famous and very popular tourist area of Austria (the Salzkammergut).

We played like children.
TAUBERT. Epiphania
Aphrodisiaca! You know all the tricks.
But nevertheless …
EFFIE. I once knew a man
who had lots of ammunition and shot
in all directions if someone even tugged
the white hairs on his chest. But listen
to that song! Heiri Wipf is singing!
HEIRI WIPF. (*Up in a plum tree, singing in front of the window.*)
O the plums were so blue!
O the plums were so blue!

TAUBERT. Ah, that voice! It goes right through me!
EFFIE. (*Opening the window and calling outside.*) Dearest Heiri, stop picking all those plums!
TAUBERT. How can one possibly describe that lovely view!
When you think of it, how soon this splendor
will remain beautiful only to other souls.
EFFIE. Here plum-gathering Heiri comes in person!
HEIRI WIPF. (*Kneeling on the window ledge, a sack on his shoulders.*) That song about plums is a lovely damn song! You work like a quarryman from morning till night, but you can't for the life of you get that song out of your head!
EFFIE. Then sing it for us. Come, Heiri. Climb in,
with your sack full of plums, and sing!
HEIRI WIPF. A lovely anonymous song! It's from High Germany![1] The court jester has to sing it to the castle maiden every morning! I sing high German badly.
(*He sings.*)

O the plums are so blue, so blue!
O the plums are so blue!
Then the famers come and crush

1 *High Germany* Mountainous regions of south Germany. Since the founding of modern Austria (in 1918) the phrase is no longer common as a geographical term. The term High German or hochdeutsch refers to the dialect of the region. The word nowadays denotes standard German—i.e., the officially accepted version of German which transcends all local dialects.

all the plums in a dreadful mush.
They crush the plums so blue, so blue!
They crush the plums so blue!

TAUBERT. This stupid fool! O Effie, don't make me
have to suffer through it!

HEIRI WIPF. A stupid fool! (*Raising his fist and going after Taubert.*) For me that would be a welcome novelty. (*Taubert moves quickly out of his way.*) I am dirt. You are dirt. And the castle maiden is—she is made of the finest stuff there is. We'd all be better off if we were stupid fools.

EFFIE. Bravo, Heiri! You're a prophet!
Now go outside into the garden
and pick a basket full of large fresh pears
for us to eat tonight.

HEIRI WIPF. For the night! Yes indeed! Large fresh pears for the mistress of the castle! The night is just such a damn hot time of day!

(*Heiri Wipf exits downstage right.*)

EFFIE. Now there's the very image of a man!
TAUBERT. Epiphania Aphrodisiaca!
EFFIE. What is it, my sweet treasure?
TAUBERT. At other times,
whenever you've been in a tangled mess,
you've always acted on what I've advised.
So are we not accomplices? We two
trade in goods we simply cannot sell
to all those who consume them every day,
like their daily bread. You deal with flesh,
and I with spirit, and human beings
accept the two of us with equal rage,
because they cannot do without us both.
Epiphania, you are at a crossroads,

like Hercules[1] was once. A woman buys
her lasting happiness in life for love,
but if that does not work, then love is poison.
At that point you must let your lover go
and keep your distance from the raging beast.

EFFIE. You are a coward, just like everyone
who in his rage has thrown off priestly clothes.
My life is simply unendurable
if some adventure does not lie in wait
whose ending no one can anticipate.

TAUBERT. Only today in your two bedroom eyes
I saw no sign of any confidence.
You almost look as if you'd bumped into
some painter of a local country scene.

EFFIE. (*Breaking out in tears.*) Don't torture me! No more torturing me!
I can't go on without love in my life.

TAUBERT. Then I would even try it with a child
before I risked my love on Mister Tschamper.

SCENE 6

(*Karl Salzmann enters in a hurry downstage right, followed by Schigabet.*)

SALZMANN. (*Reacting to the sight of Effie.*) What's this? Tears? Now? Who brought this on?
(*To Taubert.*)
You stupid clumsy ox! Get out of here!

SCHIGABET. (*Agitated and walking around, to Salzmann.*) You kept ignoring me completely,
as if I was your valet.[2] A gentleman
at festive celebrations does not strive

1 *like Hercules* The mythological Greek hero Hercules is said to have been visited in his youth by two allegorical figures representing virtue—attained through hardships and struggle—and worldly pleasures and vice. According to this myth, he chose the former.

2 *valet* Gentleman's personal servant.

so earnestly to keep a waiting servant
at a distance. For you my rank is this—
Singer of Opera for the Ducal Court
in Bernburg. Take good note of that!
You have no contractual right at all
to treat me as if I were beneath you.

SALZMANN. (*To Effie.*) Tonight we hold a large gala banquet
in the Hall of Knights. The passageway
across the courtyard from the gallery
into the hall will be lit by torches,
candelabras blazing fire. In lime trees
on the old citadel we'll have lights,
three hundred burning paper lanterns!
And you dare show us tear-stained eyes!

EFFIE. (*Cheerful.*) But only
by way of contrast, that's all. Raindrops
smile more joyfully basking in the sun.

SALZMANN. I said I would look after your affairs
provided you remained a prostitute.
If you're a girl who likes to whine or moan,
then find yourself another manager!

TAUBERT. Epiphania, those fears I spoke of—
they now seem to me almost ridiculous.

SALZMANN. Fears? When you know every trick in the book,
there's nothing you need be afraid of!
(*To Taubert and Schigabet.*)
You two,
get yourselves out of here! Now!

SCHIGABET. You boor—don't count on me to recommend you
if the press out there asks me what you're up to.

SALZMANN. (*Pushes Schigabet and Taubert to the door downstage right.*) Whatever happens, don't recommend me
to anyone at all. I urge you not to.
Our hands are full—we have enough to do.
The more our bookings grow, the less precise
our work becomes.
(*Calling to them through the door.*)
Good merchandise, good prices.

That's my motto!

(*He goes straight across the room, opens the door in the back wall and calls.*)

Would you please come in, sir?

(*Salzmann lets Mister Tschamper enter and then disappears into the room at the back.*)

Scene 7

(*Tschamper is a gigantic figure. He has no beard and close-cropped gray hair. He takes off his top hat as he enters.*)

TSCHAMPER. You understand, my child, I intend to die.
EFFIE. Will you die today?
TSCHAMPER. As quickly as I can.
EFFIE. Good. Then I'll go now and take my clothes off.
TSCHAMPER. That is not necessary.
EFFIE. Forgive me,
but, according to the contract, you desired
to die gazing at a naked woman.
TSCHAMPER. How could you manage to misinterpret that?
It was the soul that was to be exposed.
How long is it that you have been for sale?
EFFIE. Five years. My profession suits me well.
How long have you been a customer of ours?
TSCHAMPER. As long as the world has been in place,
I've been your most devoted client.
EFFIE. So old and yet so enterprising still.
Still like a student, eager for applause.
I'm pleased we've had a chance to meet.
TSCHAMPER. As the Lord says, the pleasure is all mine.
If that were not the case, I would not pay
such sums of money to amuse myself.
EFFIE. That was premature. You had no idea
what gives me pleasure. If I love you,
is that your loss?
TSCHAMPER. We are doing business.

I have no wish to change what we've agreed.
EFFIE. A woman's business is always with the man—
in the finest marriages it's like that, too.
TSCHAMPER. And yet in marriages one rarely sees
a contract like the one Karl Salzmann made.
EFFIE. But nonetheless it's not so easy
to throw away its fetters.
TSCHAMPER. Such superstitions
help the foolish lull themselves to sleep,
those idiots who all their lives drag lust
bound up in chains of marriage.
EFFIE. Do you believe
there are such fools?
TSCHAMPER. Most people are like that.
They have no idea that in their marriage
they each retain their freedom and every day
can do and leave alone what pleases them.
EFFIE. A lovely and intoxicating thought,
but in reality each person wonders
if marriage comes from Heaven or from Hell.
TSCHAMPER. Because we need that violent conflict
between heaven and hell for our digestion.
EFFIE. That contract Salzmann made between us—
can it not also serve for just that purpose?
TSCHAMPER. No, that can't be done. The comparison
of Salzmann with a devil will not hold.
EFFIE. So am I then more closely bound to you
than people are in marriage?
TSCHAMPER. I hope so.
For the money I paid to purchase you
two-thirds of all the marriages in the world
would let themselves be torn asunder.
EFFIE. Then use your time with me as your heart wishes.
TSCHAMPER. That's unavoidable. I'm seeking death.
EFFIE. I'm pleased to offer all my expertise
to lighten your farewell.
TSCHAMPER. As you well know,

that's what you're paid to do.

EFFIE. No customer
has ever known me to break a contract.
For that I am too proud of this profession,
a career I chose myself.

TSCHAMPER. (*Sitting down at a table.*) Of course,
I'm counting on the best scenario,
when, without assistance, my suicide
will suddenly take place. That's the reason
I always carry with me a small glass
of prussic acid.[1] With your permission,
I'll pour some tiny droplets in this cup.

(*He pours a few drops out of a small bottle into the golden goblet, which is on the table.*)

EFFIE. And you still prefer I keep my clothes on?
That is not chivalrous. A prostitute,
once her vanity is hurt, is helpless,
as stupid, dumb, and clumsy as a child.

TSCHAMPER. That's how helpless I require you to be.

EFFIE. Allow me to dilute that drink a little.

(*She fills the cup with water and throws the contents out of the window.*)

TSCHAMPER. You have been married, too?

EFFIE. For two years
I put up with it. But our emotions
had no desire to live in harmony.

TSCHAMPER. (*Taking the goblet from her.*) Where did you get this cup?

EFFIE. From my lover.
He gave it to me.

TSCHAMPER. (*Pours a drop of prussic acid into the goblet and then adds water.*) I'll pour in the water we need myself.

1 *prussic acid* Hydrogen cyanide, a naturally occurring substance (also synthetically produced since the 1890s) which has many industrial uses and is also a lethal agent often used in human suicides.

(*He holds the goblet in his hand.*)

EFFIE. (*Suddenly decisive.*) Then I'll take off my clothes.
TSCHAMPER. I forbid you to.
When my mind's in torment, nervous tension
makes me strong. Don't keep showing yourself off!
EFFIE. You long to be disgusted with the world—
but you'll not get there with such self-denial.
TSCHAMPER. The flesh has its own spirit. Once the nerves
in this living creature become so tense
I feel I am a man, in that moment
I will drain this cup. And then the world
will be well rid of me.
EFFIE. (*Going cautiously up to him and stroking him in a friendly way.*)
But nonetheless,
I'll bet you scarcely know our ten-stage scale.
TSCHAMPER. Is that patented?
EFFIE. I'll name the stages for you.
TSCHAMPER. What is the lowest stage?
EFFIE. First in darkness, second lit by lamps
The cruellest suffering for slavish tramps.
TSCHAMPER. I don't belong there. The highest stage!
EFFIE. Ninth in competition, tenth sacrificial rite,
so that we never lose our sacred light.
TSCHAMPER. In competition! Lovely! That's my case exactly!
But now, instead of poetry, let's talk
about reality. Explain to me
the saddest thing in your entire life!
EFFIE. I can't do that! It's quite impossible!
All my limbs are quivering already.

(*Tschamper gets up, still holding the goblet, and pushes on the electric button close to the middle door.*)

TSCHAMPER. To cheat me of a hundred thousand dollars
is no game for children.
EFFIE. I did not choose this job
to talk about distressing things. My task

is to serve you happiness!
TSCHAMPER. One can deceive oneself.

(*Salzmann enters from the back room. Tschamper turns to address him.*)

TSCHAMPER. You need to start a bankruptcy proceeding.
This creature will not tell the saddest thing
she's ever lived through in her life.

(*Salzmann moves very close to Effie with an expression of urgency.*)

SALZMANN. Tomorrow should I show the man you love
the door—make him give up the monarchy.
Think of the scandal and the shame.

(*As Salzmann leaves he turns to Tschamper.*)

SALZMANN. She'll speak—
and say whatever there is to say.

(*Salzmann exits into the back room.*)

EFFIE. (*To Tschamper; she is trembling.*) What story then?
TSCHAMPER. (*Sitting down again at the table.*) The most depressing thing
you've ever lived through.
EFFIE. The first time I broke
my marriage vow—that was the very worst.
TSCHAMPER. Amazing! How did that happen? Explain!
EFFIE. (*Getting closer to Tschamper, confidingly.*) Isn't it the case that you'd be better off
if you seized a useful opportunity
to change from being a poor monstrosity
to become instead the happiest guest
in all the world at a feast of celebration?
TSCHAMPER. Where is this favorable opportunity?
EFFIE. Don't look too far afield!
Unnaturalness is a labyrinth,

which thousands have by now escaped.
One has to laugh and dance on air.
For failure always needs a pair.
The weirdest misfit of them all,
whom our officials label mad,
did you ever hear a person claim
I could not make him sane again?
His only suffering before
was cheerless agonies of love,
and afterwards he sometimes laughs
at how unnatural he used to be.
For now, pursuing harmless thrills,
he battles bravely through life's ills.

TSCHAMPER. Describe for me your first adultery.

EFFIE. (*Beginning to tremble.*) We suffered from the curse of boredom.
No young girl has ever known
more happiness—my husband was
the handsomest young officer
in the equestrian school,
and since the time of our first kiss
we shared a common thought—
each one had to love the other
with all the strength we had.
But though our love was strong,
our boredom swelled up like a sore.
So then he offered me advice—
to save our harmony from danger
I should seduce a stranger,
and I, like someone quite obsessed
at finding things to talk about,
flung all his money here and there,
but he didn't even seem to care.
Unable to forget his dream
he could not stop advising me
to go behind his back, betray him
with some conceited well-dressed fop
as a way to make the boredom stop.

TSCHAMPER. Did that not give you pleasure?
EFFIE. What in me was strong
for one year long
during a single night,
disappeared from sight.
Lonely desert, empty heart!
From power of will
no sense of thrill,
and everywhere both far and near,
all things seemed so crudely clear.
Depressed, I thought of earlier days—
"You threw your happiness away
to bring dead nerves back into play."
TSCHAMPER. You've told that to a hundred men already.
EFFIE. As if I couldn't tell them funnier tales!
TSCHAMPER. Your husband was then keen for you to leave.
EFFIE. No, no. Precisely the reverse.
His mind was quite resolved
to offer me to other men
to heighten his own pleasure,
and every time I was untrue
he found me twice as beautiful.
He never showed a trace of grief.
So in the end I took on any man
whom I could get into my hand.
I kept my satellites in play
to guard my body from decay,
while, wracked with hunger, my soul died.
The final remnants of our love
made their escape and flew away.
With him I acted as I would
with any wretched relative
one can't allow to die.
I hurled his money to the winds
and always hoped that in the end
he'd come to find you hateful
and fly away from you like sin.
But he's a barnacle and sticks,

until we're facing destitution,
then kills himself, drops down dead,
afraid of poverty, in my own bed.

TSCHAMPER. After three days you did not find his death
distressing, so how does such a story
give me sufficient strength for suicide?
I want cries from the heart! What about parents?
Are yours still alive?

EFFIE. Only my mother.

TSCHAMPER. How did your father die?

EFFIE. (*Reacting with shock.*) I won't talk of that!

TSCHAMPER. How did your father die? Tell me how he died!

EFFIE. I can't.

TSCHAMPER. Tell me!

EFFIE. (*Throwing her arms around his neck.*) Come away with me!
Let's not stay here. And afterwards there'll be no need
to ask me anything about my father's death
or how my husband killed himself.

TSCHAMPER. Who's paying for this?
You or me?

EFFIE. You! You're the one who's paying!

TSCHAMPER. Me? Then tell me about your father's death.

EFFIE. (*With mounting distress.*)
It was in the morning, New Year's Eve.
Snow had fallen. They came to us,
Medical Staff Officer Korff
and Major von Falkenstein.
They entered from the garden, and I,
still in a short frock, went out to meet them.
O look, these gentlemen, cheerful as ever,
have by some mistake forgotten father.
Without a word, they signaled
I should move away, as mother
came in from the breakfast room.
Major von Falkenstein, curt and dull,
"Madam, you must be calm.
Whoever trusts in God …"
Tears were rolling down his face.

Mother screams,
"But he's alive! He's still alive!"
The Major trembles.
No words at all.

TSCHAMPER. Did your father fall victim to a stroke
while visiting someone of your profession?

EFFIE. (*Crying out.*) No! He was killed fighting a duel!

TSCHAMPER. How genuine and full the feelings are,
how they still thrive, in this old world.
America and all the British Empire
could not summon up so much emotion.
Once more I have to paint myself a picture.
What is your earliest memory of your parents?
Quickly!

EFFIE. Beside the green-banked oleander tree,
mother and father sit, side by side.
I'm with them, standing on their knees.
All of a sudden I see them kissing.
I throw my arms around them both—
to me their kissing brought pure joy—
and cried we must stay this way forever,
so they could just continue kissing.

TSCHAMPER. But do you still remember your parents
fighting, cursing, striking one another?

EFFIE. That is not true! I never witnessed that!
I can't ... I can't control myself ... childhood,
my parents' house! If you had never lived
then life would be confusion, madness—
stupefying horror!

(*She is shaking, gripped by attacks of weeping.*)

TSCHAMPER. Put the handkerchief away!
Stand up! Is this all tension in your nerves?

(*He throws over a chair standing nearby and kicks it against the wall.*)

Listen to your father! Talk to him!
Answer your father! Tell your father

what you've been doing since he lay dead,
in his coffin there, in the morning,
on New Year's Eve.

EFFIE. Leave my father out of it.
My father's dead.

(*She throws herself on Tschamper and kisses him with wild passion.*)

Were you ever kissed like this?
Or this? Or this? Or this?

TSCHAMPER. Yes, for a dollar!
Now earn the hundred thousand I am paying!
You must earn it! Must I show you the way?

(*He seizes the cup and seems to take a drink.*)

EFFIE. (*With an involuntary cry.*) No! You have to live!

TSCHAMPER. You feeble creature!
Cannot watch a person die. Not even you!

EFFIE. (*Passionately.*) Because I love you! Have a man and woman
ever found themselves so suitable
for one another as you and me?
For the very first time, my existence
does not grin at me from empty sockets.

TSCHAMPER. (*Apparently exhausted.*) A memory is creeping over me,
as if I had already died in here,
within these walls.

(*He looks out the window.*)

This panoramic view
of villages clothed in such greenery,
the serrated wall leading from the bastion
to the watchtower, trees full of plums ...
My death is child's play, when what it contains
outweighs the contents of my life.

EFFIE. (*Pressing up against him affectionately.*) My love, accept your life—you haven't lived
until today.

TSCHAMPER. Neither have you.

EFFIE. I would never have become a whore

if I'd had someone there to tame me
the way you do.
TSCHAMPER. Did you search for me?
A courageous person looks for someone
to subdue her.
EFFIE. (*Twisting out of his embrace, speaking very passionately.*)
You need a woman
who will sacrifice everything for you,
and I require a man for whose sake
I would sacrifice myself.
TSCHAMPER. And you, my child,
do you believe you are a woman like that?
EFFIE. If you have any doubts my pride demands
I drink what's in this cup.
TSCHAMPER. I have my doubts.

(*Effie quickly grabs the goblet, drinks it down in a gulp, and lets it fall. Then without a sound she raises her arms, bends convulsively back, and sinks to the floor. Lying on her back, with her arms and legs bent backwards as far as possible, she throws herself silently from side to side, until her body, resting on her bent back, hands, and feet, arches upward. Then convulsions begin. These gradually become less frequent, until she remains lying there motionless.*)

Ah, that's beautiful! Yes, quite wonderful!
Thank you, my child. Thank you. No woman
has ever been so sweet!

(*He gets up and looks out the window.*)

This glorious piece of earth!
Did the knights ever dream of tournaments
taking place today in their old castle?
How odd it is—no whore can ever feel
the way most normal children tend to do
and think she's better than her parents' home.
Many of them have endured your fate.

(*He opens the door to the back room.*)

My car!

Scene 8

SALZMANN. (*Entering the room.*) To me it looks as if you've failed again.

TSCHAMPER. I hoped I had reached my goal, but then,
right under my nose, she drank the poison.

SALZMANN. Too bad! The cars are ready at the central gate.

TSCHAMPER. We were chatting—a harmless conversation
about her parents' home. Why is it no whore
can bear that? The world and I are incompatible.
The world must change.

SALZMANN. Of course, it has to change—
and it does change as quickly as it can.
But how can I make up my losses here?

TSCHAMPER. You simply have to come to Atakama
to manage my affairs.

SALZMANN. I'm a family man,
and not well-suited for adventures.

TSCHAMPER. I'll pay you—
a fixed salary of fifty thousand dollars
and a hundred thousand yearly profit
guaranteed.

SALZMANN. That's something to consider.

(*Opening the small arched door downstage left.*)

Let's walk down the tower. A rocky cleft
provides a hidden path to the central gate.

TSCHAMPER. (*Picking the goblet up from the floor.*) I'll take this with me as a souvenir.

(*He exits downstage left. Salzmann follows him.*)

HEIRI WIPF. (*Singing offstage, outside the window.*) O the plums were so blue!

In Context

Presented here is a short selection of materials to help contextualize the socio-cultural significance of Wedekind's work in turn-of-the-century Germany. On the one hand, Wedekind was writing at a time when sexual science, in conjunction with psychoanalysis, emerged globally as a discipline; on the other hand, the political and moral landscape of Germany in the Kaiserreich met Wedekind's provocations with censorship, performance bans, and temporary incarceration of the author.

from Richard von Krafft-Ebing, *Psychopathia Sexualis* (1886)[1]

The driving force of sexuality, non-normative and otherwise, plays a prominent role not only in *Castle Wetterstein* but also in much of Wedekind's other work. Nineteenth-century psychiatrist and sexologist Richard von Krafft-Ebing's *Psychopathia Sexualis* (1886) is a central work in the early stages of modern sexuality studies. Ideas from his writings soon began to transcend their medical context and to permeate legal discourses, early feminist discourses, and literary production in fin-de-siècle Europe. Krafft-Ebing situates his own medical-scientific approach here on an imagined middle-ground between literature and poetry on the one hand, and philosophical treatises on love on the other hand; he references the work of the German philosopher Arthur Schopenhauer, whose views on sexuality and romance were notoriously pessimistic. Krafft-Ebing frames his discussions of sexual deviance and immorality with generalizations about society as a whole that are also relevant to Wedekind, who made no secret (either in his public statements or in his satirical writings) of his disdain for modern society.

---

1 Translated by Charles Gilbert Craddock (1894). This edition is an "Authorized Translation of the Seventh Enlarged and Revised German Edition of *Psychopathia Sexualis.*" It has been chosen for its contemporaneity with Wedekind's early dramas which address the topos of sexuality. Numerous other, later translations exist, some of which may better reflect nuances of the German original.

The poets may be better psychologists than the psychologists and philosophers; but they are men of feeling rather than of understanding, and at least one-sided in their consideration of the subject. They cannot see the deep shadow behind the light and sunny warmth of that from which they draw their inspiration. The poetry of all times and nations would furnish inexhaustible material for a monograph on the psychology of love; but the great problem can be solved only with the help of Science, and especially with the aid of Medicine, which studies the psychological subject at its anatomical and physiological source, and views it from all sides.

Perhaps it will be possible for medical science to gain a standpoint of philosophical knowledge midway between the despairing views of philosophers like Schopenhauer and Hartmann, and the gay, *naïve* views of the poets.

Sexuality is the most powerful factor in individual and social existence; the strongest incentive to the exertion of strength and acquisition of property, to the foundation of a home, and to the awakening of altruistic feelings, first for a person of the opposite sex, then for the offspring, and, in a wider sense, for all humanity.

Periods of moral decadence in the life of a people are always contemporaneous with times of effeminacy, sensuality, and luxury. These conditions can only be conceived as occurring with increased demands upon the nervous system, which must meet these requirements. As a result of increase of nervousness, there is increase of sexuality, and, since this leads to excesses among the masses, it undermines the foundation of society,—the morality and purity of family life. When this is destroyed by excesses, unfaithfulness, and luxury, then the destruction of the state is inevitably composed in material, moral, and political ruin. Warning examples of this character are presented by Rome, Greece, and France under Louis XIV and XV. In such times of political and moral destruction monstrous perversions of the sexual life were frequent, which, however, may in part be referred to psycho-pathological, or, at least, neuro-pathological conditions existing in the people.

from Frank Wedekind, *The Censors. Theodicee in One Act* (1907)[1]

In *The Censors*, a powerful autobiographical work, Wedekind presents a thinly veiled representation of the actual censorship he endured at the hands of German officials—and a broader agenda of exposing the workings of oppressive societal mechanisms. The German *Zensurbehörde* (State Office of Censorship) is represented by a character named "Dr. Prantl," who visits an author named Buridan and his actress wife Kadidja (alter egos of Wedekind and his wife Tilly) in an earlier scene. The scene selected here takes place immediately after the unwanted visitor's departure. The two protagonists engage in a dialogue that touches on the themes of censorship, artistic freedom, the hypocrisy of marriage, and the sexual ethos of the times.

Third Scene

KADIDJA:[2] (still standing on the running drum[3]): What did the gentleman want?

BURIDAN (on the diwan): The gentleman wanted to bid me farewell forever. (He picks up the book from the floor and leafs through the pages.)

KADIDJA: The parting seems to affect you greatly.—If it were me, you would let me go more easily.—Do you still remember the endless row of coffins, which you had drawn in your notebook?

BURIDAN (without looking at her): Yes, I do remember the coffins.

KADIDJA: On every single coffin, you had written the words: Alone, finally.

---

1 Translated from the German original by Nisha Kommattam.

2 *KADIDJA* The Arabic name of this protagonist (assumed to be his wife Tilly's alter ego), was also Wedekind's daughter's name in real life.

3 *running drum* A cylindric device commonly used by circus artists and acrobats as a means of locomotion.

BURIDAN: Alone, finally.

KADIDJA: And if I now truly wanted to leave you?

BURIDAN: You wouldn't believe how fervently my soul longs for that state of affairs!

KADIDJA: But aren't those words originally referring to *two* people, who were finally alone together, in their *nuptial chamber*?

BURIDAN (without looking up): These words will change again in meaning for those two as well.

KADIDJA: Don't you want to look at me? (Since Buridan is not replying:) I am standing on your running drum here.—I am standing here in the fancy-dress costume which I am supposed to be wearing tomorrow evening, in the wedding ballet, in the performance of your play.

BURIDAN: I am searching in vain for an expression that shows how endlessly indifferent I am about tomorrow's performance of my play.

KADIDJA: Poor Buridan!—(She jumps off the running drum.) What else is supposed to spark joy in you, when your own theater plays fail to do so! (She sits down on his knee.) Please do not feel startled by this. I, too, am merely here to bid you farewell.—I will now venture back out, onto the wild open sea on which you captured me eighteen months ago; on which one can only stay afloat thanks to one's own strengths and advantages. With you, I could now only stay afloat by virtue of my faults—assuming, of course, that I had any.

BURIDAN: For some time now, I have been thinking about opening a brothel as an institution of moral education. A house in which the pupils grow so weary of pleasure over the years that they will thenceforth, for the rest of their lives, regard what others consider woe and worry as their highest pleasure.

KADIDJA (rises and kneels down on the diwan next to him): You truly seem to be destined by the heavens to ruin the greatest pleasures in life for your fellow man.

BURIDAN: You don't understand that one becomes an object of revulsion, when only eating and drinking and loving for one's own sake.

KADIDJA: But wouldn't this pleasure be man enough to overcome such disgust?

BURIDAN: Why do caged wild beasts not love?—Because they lack the freedom to hunt down their prey.

KADIDJA: I lack that freedom just as much, and yet I do love.

BURIDAN: Your love feels as free as my vigor lies chained.—What am I?—What am I?

KADIDJA: Well? (She steps towards the mirror.) And I am supposed to be an angel!

from Frank Wedekind, Letter to Georg Brandes (1901)[1]

Wedekind's correspondence was vast, and much of it survives. This letter makes a direct statement about the significance of *Castle Wetterstein*. Georg Brandes (1842–1927) was an influential Scandinavian literary scholar and critic in turn-of-the-century Europe. Throughout the years in which Wedekind faced censorship and persecution from the German authorities, he remained in lively intellectual and artistic communication with many of the prominent thinkers and artists of his time—among them Bertolt Brecht, Heinrich and Thomas Mann, and Stefan Zweig.

Lenzburg, County Aargau, Switzerland August 27th 1910

Venerated Master!
Dear Professor!

Our common friend, Mr. Arthur Landsberger, has encouraged me to submit to you my three most recent one-act plays. Since I do not carry any copies with me here in my summer resort, I have instructed my publisher to send them to you. I trust you will not consider it immodest or inartistic of me to make a few comments on them—comments I withhold from the audience. The three single-act plays are nothing else than one drama in three acts, which I have intermittently published one act after another, since the German critics had declared me artistically dead and completely sterile. The play is titled "Castle Wetterstein, A Family Trilogy." The first act, which was published most recently, is: "Firm in all Saddles" [In allen Sätteln gerecht]. The second act is: "Hunted by all Hounds" [Mit allen Hunden gehetzt]. The third act, which I had published first, is: "With Every Trick in the Book" [Mit allen Wassern gewaschen].

In the first act, with the utmost reverence I have taken the liberty of tying onto Ibsen's family dramas. For everything I had to say in the three acts were my personal experiences of [the sorts

1 Translated from the German original by Nisha Kommattam.

of] family problems described by Ibsen. The fact that all material things, all events were mere pretexts for me, smokescreens allowed me to freely speak of my convictions, will be unforgivable for you, my dear Mr. Brandes, as a pioneer of honorable art. This is also the reason why I freely admit to you what I would never confess to the audience, to critics or literary scholars. Please do not consider it an empty phrase, if I prefer being understood by you to my disadvantage but correctly, rather than being misunderstood in my favor. If you consider my frankness to be pride, I cannot object. But perhaps my veneration for your work, and the gratitude that I have been feeling towards you for almost thirty years now, will outweigh this sentiment. [...]

Your most obedient servant,

Frank Wedekind

Images

Frank Wedekind in his study, 1890s.

Wedekind on stage, performing his own play *Erdgeist* (*Earth Spirit*), in 1898.

Im heiligen Land

Der König David steigt aus seinem Grabe,
Greift nach der Harfe, schlägt die Augen ein,
Und preist den Herrn, daß er die Ehre habe,
Dem Herrn der Völker einen Psalm zu weihn.
Wie einst zu Abisags von Sunem*) Tagen
Hört wieder man ihn wild die Saiten schlagen,
Indeß sein hehres Preis- und Siegeslied
Wie Sturmesbrausen nach dem Meere zieht.

Willkommen, Fürst, in meines Landes Grenzen,
Willkommen mit dem holden Ehgemahl,
Mit Geistlichkeit, Lakaien, Excellenzen,
Und Polizeibeamten ohne Zahl.
Es freuen rings sich die histor'schen Orte
Seit vielen Wochen schon auf deine Worte,
Und es vergrößert ihre Sehnsuchtspein
Der heiße Wunsch, photographiert zu sein.

Ist denn nicht deine Herrschaft auch so weise,
Daß du dein Land getrost verlassen kannst?
Nicht jeder Herrscher wagt sich auf die Reise
Ins alte Kanaan. Du aber fandst,
Du seist zu Hause momentan entbehrlich;
Der Augenblick ist völlig ungefährlich;
Und wer sein Land so klug wie du regiert,
Weiß immer schon im Voraus, was passiert.

Es wird die rote Internationale,
Die einst so wild und ungebärdig war,
Versöhnen sich beim sanften Liebesmahle
Mit der Agrarier sanftgemuten Schar.
Frankreich wird seinen Dreyfus froh empfangen,
Als wär auch er zum heilgen Land gegangen.
In Peking wird kein Kaiser mehr vermißt,
Und Ruhe hält sogar der Anarchist.

So sei uns denn noch einmal hochwillkommen
Und laß dir unsre tiefste Ehrfurcht weihn,
Der du die Schmach vom heilgen Land genommen,
Von dir bisher noch nicht besucht zu sein.
Mit Stolz erfüllst du Millionen Christen;
Wie wird von nun an Golgatha sich brüsten,
Das einst vernahm das letzte Wort vom Kreuz
Und heute nun das erste deinerseits.

Der Menschheit Durst nach Thaten läßt sich
stillen,
Doch nach Bewundrung ist ihr Durst enorm.
Der du ihr beide Durste zu erfüllen
Vermagst, seis in der Tropen-Uniform,
Sei es in Seemannstracht, im Purpurkleide,
Im Rokoko-Kostüm aus starrer Seide,
Sei es im Jagdrock oder Sportgewand,
Willkommen, teurer Fürst, im heilgen Land!

Hieronymos

*) I. Könige I, 1–4.

Berlin W.

(Zeichnung von E. Thöny)

„Wozu reisen de Leut' nach Palästina?"

— 245 —

Wedekind's poem "Im Heiligen Land" ("In the Holy Land") was published in 1898 under the pseudonym "Hieronymus" in the satirical journal *Simplicissimus.* (See the introduction, page 10.)

Frank Wedekind and his wife Tilly (*née* Newes, 1886–1970) as newlyweds in 1906.

Frank and Tilly Wedekind posing for the magazine "Berliner Leben," [Berlin Life] 1910.

From the Publisher

A name never says it all, but the word "Broadview" expresses a good deal of the philosophy behind our company. We are open to a broad range of academic approaches and political viewpoints. We pay attention to the broad impact book publishing and book printing has in the wider world; for some years now we have used 100% recycled paper for most titles. Our publishing program is internationally oriented and broad-ranging. Our individual titles often appeal to a broad readership too; many are of interest as much to general readers as to academics and students.

Founded in 1985, Broadview remains a fully independent company owned by its shareholders—not an imprint or subsidiary of a larger multinational.

For the most accurate information on our books (including information on pricing, editions, and formats) please visit our website at www.broadviewpress.com. Our print books and ebooks are also available for sale on our site.

broadview press
www.broadviewpress.com

This book is made of paper from well-managed FSC® - certified forests, recycled materials, and other controlled sources.

MIX
Paper from responsible sources
FSC® C103567
www.fsc.org

PCF

BIO GAS ENERGY

PERMANENT